GENERAL AGRICULTURE

FOR ICAR'S EXAMS, JRF, SRF, ARS & IARI PH. D. EXAMS
(BASED ON AUTHORIZED AND CURRENT INFORMATION)

DR. SATWIK SAHAY BISARYA

Contents

Preface

Agriculture is the backbone of Indian economy. In India, the competition in agricultural education is increasing day by day. The competitive examination is an only routine procedure of admission in Agricultural Universities, viz. Central Agriculture University (CAU), State Agricultural Universities (SAUs), Indian Agricultural Research Institute (IARI). The competitive examination is also an only routine procedure of recruitment in agricultural job/posts, viz. Agricultural Research Services, State PSC and UPSC. Thus, one has to prepare him/herself very strongly for these competition exams and for the success, need to read authentic and authorised reading materials. The knowledge of general agriculture is very essential for every competition exams related to agriculture. Many authors are attempted to compile the notes/books of general agriculture. Other books were also made impact on the readers. But still no book is there with authentic and authorised information. Therefore, I and my friends feel need to write this book. This book has been so as to serve, as best as possible to aim of writing this book.

Here, I would like to express my heartfelt thanks to the person who prepared the notes with his /her hard work. I am highly thankful to Mr. Ajit Kumar who helped me for material collection and typing. Finally, I wish to thank all the friends, who encouraged me to compile this book, Deepak Baboo, Raj Kumar, Arvind Kumar. And also thanks to other friends for there, cooperation, Anupma, Bandana, Sanjay.

References:

1. Handbook of Agriculture- ICAR (new edition)
2. General Agriculture- Muni raj Singh (new edition)
3. Economic Survey of India- Govt. of India (2009-10)
4. India-2010
5. ICAR websites
6. TNAU notes
7. Fundamentals of Soil Science-ISSS

Authors Affilation

Dr. Satwik Sahay Bisarya, Assosiat Professor, Facalty of Agriculture Science and Technology, Madhyanchal Professional University, Bhopal

Dr. Deepak Baboo, Assistant Professor, Facalty of Agriculture Science and Technology, Madhyanchal Professional University, Bhopal

Maya Bisen, Assistant Professor, Facalty of Agriculture Science and Technology, SAGE University, Indor

Ayushi Singh, Assistant Professor, Facalty of Agriculture Science and Technology, SAM Globel University, Bhopal

CHAPTER ONE

INDIAN AGRICULTURE: AT A GLANCE

1. *Indian Agriculture:*

- A record production of 233.88 Million tons of food grains in 2008-09
- Contribution to Growth rate in GDP – 4.7% (2007-08), 1.6% (2008-09)
- Contribution to GDP –16.4 % (2007-08), 15.7% (2008-09)
- Share to total imports– 2.95% (2007-08), 2.74% (2008-09)
- Share to total exports – 12.05% (2007-08), 10.23% (2008-09)
- Contribution to total Employment- 52% (2008-09)
- India supports(of world's):

  - Total geographical area-2%
  - population- 18%
  - Livestock-15%
  - Forest-1.5%

- Total Geographical Area (TGA) - 329 M.H
- Potential for Biological Production - 265 M.H
- Per Capita land availability-0.37ha (1991-92)
- Per Capita Agri. land availability -0.16 ha(1991-92)
- Net cultivated area- 143 Mha

- Irrigated area-56.3 Mha
- National Commission on Farmers-2004 (Chairman- M.S. Swaminathan)
- National Horticulture Mission-started 2005
- National Bamboo Mission-started 2006-07
- NRAA- National Rain fed Area Authority, since 03/11/2006
- National food security mission-started Rabi, 2007
- RADP- Rain fed Area Development Programme, Since 20 March, 2008
- All India avg. fertilizer consumption- 128.8 Kg/ha (2008-09)
- Highest avg. fertilizer consumption- Punjab (212Kg/ha)
- Lowest avg. fertilizer consumption – Arunachal Pradesh (5 kg/ha)
- Nutrient consumption ration (NPK), 2007-08)- 5.5:2.1:1
- NPMSF- National Project on Management of Soil Health & Fertilizer, 2008-09
- ISOPOM-Integrated Scheme of Oilseeds, Pulses, Oil palm & Maize, started since 1st April, 2004
- Kisan Call Centre(KCC),started since 21st Jan 2004 (toll free No. 1551)
- DMRI- Directorate of Marketing Research and Inspection, Nagpur , Maharashtra
- First livestock census conducted in India: 1919
- Rank of India in Silk production-2nd (1st-China), - 18,320 MT
- Provides about 65% of the livelihood
- Contributes 21% of Total Exports, and Supplies Raw materials to Industries
- Growth Rate in production - 5.8%
- About 75% people are living in rural areas and are still dependent on Agriculture.
- About 43% of India's geographical area is used for agricultural activity.

General Agriculture (New, ICAR wbsites):

- Sahbhagi Dhan - new varieties of rice capable of withstanding drought.
- Water submergence variety of rice- Swarna-Sub 1, can survive for 14 days under water.
- To ward off threat to wheat production from the globally spreading menace of resistant varieties of wheat stem rust- Ug99,DBW 17, PBW 550, Lok 1, and Turja identified.
- In potato, dry matter-rich variety Kufri Frysona developed for making French Fries.
- Cloned and surviving buffalo calf, GARIMA, produced for faster multiplication of selected highly productive animals.
- For Bird Flu diagnosis, High Security Animal Disease Laboratory, Bhopal, conferred OIE-international recognition.
- Devised drip and sprinkler irrigation systems saving water (30-50%), labour (50%), fertilizer (30-40%) and increasing yields (12-76%).
- Leaf Colour Chart (LCC), a simple device for nitrogen management saves 15 kg N/ha in rice.
- Tractor-mounted cumin planter saves 30% seed.
- Motorized aril extractor developed for pomegranate.
- The first systematic work on SRI began at TNAU, Tamil Nadu in 1993.
- Golden rice: Produced by combining genetic material from daffodils, *Ervinia vredivora*, *Agrobacterium tumifacience* and Japonica rice. by Professor Ingo Potrykus and Dr. Peter Beyer (Germany,1999)
- Purpose of golden rice- to provide a new, alternative intervention to combat Vitamin A Deficiency.

General Agriculture by Muniraj Singh (New Entry):

- National Biodiversity Board-New Delhi
- Camel crop-Sorgum
- Natural Genetic enginner-Agrobacterium tumefacience
- Pashmina (Winter cloth) obtained from- Goats

- Law of Tolerance –Sheford
- Oleresine- Chilli
- Keshar(sefforon) belongs family-Iridaceae
- World Food Prize,1987 (1st Indian)-M.S. Swaminathan for Green revolution
- World Food Prize,1989 (2nd Indian)-Vergese Kurien for Milk revolution
- World Food Prize,2000 (5th Indian)-S. K. Khus for Quality Protein Maize
- World Food Prize, 2009- Gebisa Ejeta (Ethiopia) for 1st sorghum hybrid for drought and srtiga weed.
- Mychoryza increase availability of – Phosphorus
- Water Requirement of irrigated wetland rice-1500 mm
- Nurient mobility concepts-Bray
- PUFA conent is highest in –Sunflower
- Pseudocereal-Buckwheat
- First Agri. Chemist of ICAR-J W Leather
- Pulse crop doesn't fix N-Rajma
- Avg Milling recovery of Rice-60%

Informatics in Agriculture:

- IT Plan for Agriculture Sector (AGRISNET) was submitted to Ministry of Agriculture in 1997 to establish "Indian Agriculture on-line" and revised in 2000.
- AGMARKNET-Agricultural Marketing Information Network
- NADAMS-National Agricultural Drought Advisory and Management Systems
- AgRIS-Resources Information System
- APHNET-Animal Production and Health Informatics Network
- ARISNET-Agricultural Research and Information System
- ACINET: Agricultural Credit Anformatics Network
- E-*chaupal* estabilished by Indian Tobacco Comp. (ITC) for M.P.
- VERCON (Vitrual Extension, Research and Communication Network) developed by- FAO,2001

- Soya-Chaupal is for weather, farming practice and Market price of Soybean in M.P.
- ICT- Information and Communication Technology
- ARIS- Agricultural Research Information System, est. by ICAR, 1995

Nanotechnology in Agriculture:

- coined by-Nario Taniguichi (1974), at Univ. of Tokyo, Japan
- Nanotechnology is Understanding and control of matter at dimension of 1-100 nm
- Example of Nano based Smart Delivery System-Halloysite
- Nano Pesticide-Nano Particles(NPs) of ZnO, Sio_2 and TiO_2 used for Bacteria & Green Algea
- Nano Particles used for reclamation of heavy Particles-Amphiphylic Polyurethane,Zeravalent Iron (nZVI), and Nano sized Zeolite.

Crop Biotechnology:

- First transgenic plant-Flavr Savr^{TM} tomato for delayted ripining was realeasd for commercial cultivation in 1994 by Calgene (Compony).
- Final Approval Committee for release of transgenic crops in India- GEAC (Genetic Engineering Approval Committee)
- Area under transgenic plant in World (2008)-125 Mha, 139 Mha (2009)
- Rank of India for transgenic plant -4th (1st-USA, 2nd-Mexico, 3rd-Argentina)
- Crops having highest transgenic plant cultivation area-Soyabean> Corn>Cotton
- Area under Bt-cotton: 7.5 Mha(2008), 8.4 Mha (2009)(86% of cotton area)
- First genetic engineering compony est. 1976, Genentech
- First transgenic crop- tobacco

Irrigation in India:

- National water awards (2007)-Hiware Bazar Gram Panchayat, Ahmadnagar, Mharastra
- Area under micro irrigation system in india (2008-09): 3.88 Mha
- Area under Drip in India (2008-09): 1.42 Mha (highest area-Maharashtra)
- Area under Sprinkler in India (2008-09): 2.45 Mha (highest area-Haryana)
- Water year-2007
- Artificial Recharge of Ground Water Advisory Council (ARGWC)- constituted in 2006
- National Institute of Hydrology- Roorkee, Uttarakhand
- World Congress on conservation Agriculture, 2009- held at New Delhi

ITK in Agriculture:

- Bael fruit can be used to contol –rice blast
- Cow urin used for – wheat termite control , sorghum smut control

India's position in world Agriculture	Rank
Total Area	Seventh
Irrigated Area	First
Population	Second
Economically Active population	Second
Total Cereals	Third
Wheat	Second
Rice	Second
Coarse grains	Fourth
Total Pulses	First
Oil Seeds	Second
Fruits and Vegetables	Second (first-China)
Implements (Tractors)	Third
Milk	First
Live Stock (castles, Buffaloes)	First

WORLD AGRICULTURAL SCENARIO

- **Rice** : China > India > Indonesia
- **Maize** : USA >China >Brazil
- **Wheat** : China > India >Usa
- **Groundnut** : China > India
- **Sugarcane** : Brazil > India
- **Total Cereals** : China > USA > India
- **Coarse Cereals**: Usa > China > Brazil > India
- **Total Pulses** : India -1st
- **Mustard & Rapeseed**: China > Canada > India
- **Fruits & Veg** : China > India
- **Cotton** : CHINA > USA > India
- **Tobacco** : China > Brazil > India
- **Tea, Jute & Allied Fibres**: India -1st
- **Coffee** :India-6th
- **Cattle Population**: 1st (16.5%)
- **Buffalo Population**: 1st (56.7%)
- **Milk Production**: 1st (15%)

- **Egg Production**: China>USA>Japan>India
- **Total Area of India**-329 m ha-2.4% of world-7th position
- **Total Arable Land**-162 m ha-2nd after USA
- **Total Irrigated Area**-58 m ha-21% of world-1st position
- **Human Population**-102.5 Crore-17% of world-2nd after China

INDIANS WHO SECURED WORLD FOOD PRIZES:

- 1987- Dr MS Swaminathan- architect of India's "green revolution"
- 1989-Dr Verghese Kurien – Milk cooperatives
- 1996 - Dr Gurudev S Kush – improved yield potential of rice
- 1998 – Mr B R Barwale – Founder of MAHYCO
- 2000 – Dr Surinder K Vassal – Developed quality protein maize
- 2005 – Modaduga v Gupta – For Aquaculture

SOME IMPORTANT YEARS:

- 2004-International year of rice
- 2005-International year of micro credit
- 2006-International year of desert and desertification
- 2007-International year of water (theme-more crop per drop)
- 2008-International year of potato
- 2009-International year of fibre
- 2010- International year of Biodiversity

PER CAPITA AVAILABILITY

- Cereals – 409.9 gm/day
- Pulse -29 gm/day
- Milk - 245 gm /day.
- Minimum requirement of milk – 240 gm/day

World Green Revolution:

- Increasing the wheat production that began in Mexico in 1945.
- The term "Green Revolution" was first used in 1968 by former USAID director William Gaud.
- CIMMYT , Mexico - the International Maize and Wheat Improvement Center.
- Green Revolution was the production of novel wheat cultivars.
- HYVs or "high-yielding varieties - A Japanese dwarf wheat cultivar (Norin 10 wheat) which yield 10 times more than that of traditional rice.
- Father of the Green Revolution- Norman Ernest Borlaug (Birth- March 25, 1914 and Death - September 12, 2009 (aged 95) Dallas, Texas (USA). An American agronomist and Nobel laureate who has been deemed the. He received his Ph.D. in plant pathology and genetics.)
- Father of the Green Revolution in India- M. S. Swaminathan (Mankombu Sambasivan Swaminathan, born August 7, 1925, in Kumbakonam, Tamilnadu.)
- Father of the Ever Green Revolution in India (1995) - M. S. Swaminathan.
- Punjab was selected by the Indian government to be the first site to try the new crops for Green Revolution.
- The land Mark of Indian Green Revolution- IARI, New Delhi
- "Miracle Rice"-IR8 - a semi-dwarf rice variety developed by IRRI. Crossed between an Indonesian variety named "Peta" and a Chinese variety named "Dee-geo-woo- gen."

CROP PRODUCTION SCENARIOS IN INDIAN AGRICULTURE

:

- Total foodgrains production in 2008-09 was estimated at 233.88 million tonnes as against 230.78 million tonnes in 2007-08.

Current trends in Indian agriculture:

- 10th largest economy in terms of GDP

- 10th in world plant biodiversity (4th in Asia)
- India is in 4th position in Purchasing Power Parity (PPP)

Leading state in production and area of crops:

- Rice – WB> UP, Punjab (Productivity)
- Wheat – UP> Punjab, Haryana (productivity)
- Pulse s– MP (production), Haryana (productivity)
- Oilseed – MP>AP, TN (productivity)
- Groundnut – Gujarat (production), TN (productivity)
- Mustard – Rajasthan
- Cotton – Maharashtra
- Jute – West Bengal
- Coffee – Karnataka
- Tea – Assam
- Rubber – Kerala> Tripura
- Potato – UP
- Onion – Maharashtra
- Sugarcane – Uttar Pradesh (production), Tamil Nadu (productivity)
- Maize – Karnataka
- Soybean – MP(production), AP (productivity)

POINTS NEED TO REMEMBER

- India's rank in fertilizer consumption- 3rd
- Per ha NPK consumption-128 kg
- CV of South west Monsoon in 2009- 10%
- MSP given by CACP
- CACP stands for - Commission on Agriculture cost and Prices
- FCI Buffer stock, Oct 2009- 16.2 Mt
- Swaljaldhara is – drinking water project, 2002
- Hariyali- watershed development program est. 2003
- NAREGA changes to MAREGA (Mahatma Gandhi Rural Employment Guaranty Act) 2005

- The Protection of Plant Varieties and Farmers' Rights (PPV&FR) Authority, established in Nov., 2005 at New Delhi (Chairaman- S. Nagrajan)
- National Project on Management of Soil Health & Fertility (NPMSF), has been introduced in 2008-09
- Total No. of Soil Testing Laboratories (STLs)in India-750 (2008-09)
- Total irrigation potential in India- 102.77 million ha by March 2007
- Accelerated Irrigation Benefit Programme (AIBP) started since 1996-97
- NAFED -National Agricultural Cooperative Marketing Federation of India Limited
- CCI- Cotton Corporation of India
- The Macro Management of Agriculture Scheme (MMA) was formulated in 2000-01
- National Food Security Mission (NFSM) has been launched from the rabi 2007-08 to enhancing the production of rice, wheat and pulses by 10, 8 and 2 million tonnes respectively by the end of the Eleventh Plan
- Kisan Credit Card Scheme (KCC) was introduced in August 1998
- Rashtriya Krishi Vikas Yojana (RKVY) - launched in August 2007
- National Bamboo Mission (NBM)- commenced in 2006-07
- National Committee on Plasticulture Applications in Horticulture (NCPAH)
- Chairman, Planning Commissions- M. S. Ahuliwalia
- Chairman of National Commission for Farmers - Dr. M.S. Swaminathan
- India's Rank
- 1st- Milk, Coconut, Tea, Banana, Mango, Cashew nut (export, import and processing) and Pulses
- 2nd- Rice , Wheat, Cotton, Fruit and vegetable
- 3rd- Tobacco, rubber, Egg and fertilizer

- Consumption of Pesticide is maximum
- Imported Pesticide: Carbaryl followed by cholorpyriphos
- Indigenous Pesticide: BHC followed by Monocrotophos & Endosulfan
- Export of Agro chemicals
- Maximum (in terms of rupees): Cypermethrin followed by Endosulfan, Phosphide & Lindane
- The top Agrobusiness company: Novartis (Hindustan Ciba-Geigy & Sandoz)
- Total production of pesticides in India : 95,000 tones (2007-08)
- Number of pesticides registered in India: L55-(as on 31/12/99)
- Number of technical grade pesticides manufactured in India:
- Plant Protection adviser to GOL: Dr. R. L. RAJAK.
- Insecticides Act: 1968 (Thakur committee recommendation)
- Insecticides rules : 1971
- Brown revolution - Promotion of Agro Industries Dvt.
- Pink revolution - Promotion of onion production
- Yellow revolution - Promision of oilseeds production
- The word green revolution was coined by "William Gadd"
- Father of Green revolution Norman E. Borlaoug.
- Father of Green revolution in India Dr. M.S. Swaminathan
- Father of hybrid rice production: yuvan long ping
- First laureate of the "world food' prize: Dr. Swaminathan
- World Food prize – 1986
- Rice breeders: Dr. H. M. Beachell, Dr. Gurdev singh khush
- NCIPM – National Centre for Integrated Pest Management – IARI, New Delhi
- CPPPTI – Central Plant Protection Training Institute – Hyderabad
- The largest per hectare pesticide consuming country – Taiwan
- Total number of pesticides banned in India = 29
- Recently banned - Phosphamidon
- Highest consumption – cotton 54% followed by paddy 22%

RECENT INSECTICIDE DATA

- Number of insecticide included in insecticide schedule- 787
- Pesticides Banned for manufacture, import and use - 27
- Pesticide / Pesticide formulations banned for use but their manufacture is allowed for export - 2
- Pesticide formulations banned for import, manufacture and use - 4
- Pesticide Withdrawn - 7
- No. of pesticides refused registration - 18
- Pesticides restricted for use in India – 13
- Insecticides approved by the registration committee for protecting buildings from termites : Chlorpyriphos 50% EC, Ethion 50% EC, Imidacloprid 30.50% SC, Lindane 20% EC.
- Insecticides approved by the registration committee to control termites in agricultural crops under the insecticides act, 1968 : Chlorpyriphos 20 EC, Endosulfan 35 EC, Imidacloprid 17.8 % SL.
- No. of Insecticides approved by the registration committee to control household pests in houses under the insecticides act, 1968 - 39.

CHAPTER TWO

HORTICUTURE

Main varieties: Remarks

1. Mallika:
2. Ainrapali: HDP, Dwarfing, developed by IARI
3. Lal Sundari: Coloured variety, developed by IARI
4. Niranjan: Off season bearer
5. Mandhulika: Off season bearer
6. MDCH-2: Off season bearer
7. Arka Aruna: Free from spongy tissue
8. Arka Puneet: Free from spongy tissue
9. Arka Anmol: Free from spongy tissue
10. Arka Neelkiran:
11. Sindhu: Seedless
12. Dashehari : Best North Indian cultivar
13. Chausa: Sweeten, Very late varieties
14. Neehun:Best combiner, Very late varieties
15. Kalepadi: Dwarfing
16. Totapuri: Red small, Dwarfing

- **Propagation** : Veneer Grafting
- **Intercrops** : Papaya, Phalsa, Onion, Tomato
- **Sex forms** : Male & Female (Andromonoceious)
- **Pollinator** : Housefly
- **Maturity indices** : 1. Specific gravity (1.01-1. 02)
- **Flowering to Harvest** : 90-120 days

- **Major pest** : Hoppers
- Physiological Disorders:

1. **Malformation:**

   - Due to low temperature
   - Control by ... 1. Deblossoming, 2. Spray of NAA @ 200 ppm, 3. Resistant cultivars- Bahaduran, Aliff, Haichi, Manjeera.

2. Black tip:

   - Due to gases from brick kilns (SO_2, NO_2 and Acetylene)
   - Cultivars with more lenticels/ unit are susceptible
   - Control : Borax spray

3. **Alternate bearing** : Control: Paclobutrazol @300 ppm (or) Kutar @ 5 gm/ tree by, Soil as well as foliar spray
4. **Spongy tissue:** Convection heats
5. **Internal Fruit necrosis:** 'B' deficiency.

Cultivation/Production of Tomato:

- **Tomato** : *Lycorpersicon esculentunn,*
- **Famous as :** Wolf Apple
- **Family** : Solanacae
- **Origin** : Peru
- **Fruit type** : Bery
- **Main Nutrient :** (rich in Vit.- A)

Main Varieties:

1. Pusa ruby 6. Pusa Gaurav Processing
2. Pusa Early Dwarf 7. Arka Vikas

3. Sioux 8. Arka Saurab
4. Marglobe 9. Arka Ahuti
5. Supreme (Seln-120) 10. Arka Ashish

- **Fruit type** : Bery
- **Main Nutrient** :(rich in Vit.- A)
- Main Varieties:

1. Pusa ruby 6. Pusa Gaurav Processing
2. Pusa Early Dwarf 7. Arka Vikas
3. Sioux 8. Arka Saurab
4. Marglobe 9. Arka Ahuti
5. Supreme (Seln-120) 10. Arka Ashish

- Hybrids :

1. Arka vishal,
2. Arka vardan (Registant to nematode),
3. Vaishali (Indo-American Hybrids),
4. Rupail (Indo-American Hybrids)
5. Naveen (Indo-American Hybrids)

- **Seed rate** : Normal: 300-350 gm/ha, and (Hybrid: 70-90 gm/ ha)
- **Spacing** : 60x60 cm and 90 x 90 cm
- **Maturity** : Colour development
- **Major pest** : Fruit borer (Helicoverpa armijera)
- **Major Disease** : Tomato Spotted wilt virus (TSWV), Damping off, (Vector

Thrips)

- **BER** : Blosoom-End-Rot (due to Calcium deficiency.)
- **Cold set** : eg. Pusa sheetal, Pusa Hybrid-2
- **Hot set** : eg: Pusa Hybrid-1

Cultivation/Production of Rose:

- **B. N. :** *Rosa hybrid*
- **Family** : Rosaceae
- **Propagation** :T- budding
- **Type** : 1. Hybrid Tea: Hybrid perpetual ×Tea Rose-(Large solitary flowers)

2. Floribunda: Hybrid tea × Olyanthes – Medium flower on clusters.

- **Export Varieties:** First Red Golden Times, Mercedes, Belinda, Sonia, Milan, Red Success, B.P. Pal, Mother Teresa, Chitra.

Cultivation/Production of **Cauliflower:**

- **Edible part** :curd (Prefloral apical meristem)
- **Operation** : Blanching in cauliflower
- **Disorders :** Whiptail- Mo deficiency

Browning – Boron deficiency

- **Varieties** : Pusa snowball, Pusa katki, Pusa deepali, Early Kunwari.

General Horticulture:
Fruit types:
Type Example

1. Berries : Grapes, Guava, Phalsa, Tomato, Brinjal, Chitiles
2. Drupe : Mango, Peach, Plum, Cherry, Apricot
3. Hesperidum : Citrus
4. Amphisarca : Wood apple, Bael
5. Balusta : Pomegranate

6. Pome (false fruit) : Apple, Pear
7. Pepo : Cuarbits
8. Single seeded berry : Dates
9. Single seeded nuts : Litchi
10. Sorosis : Jack, Mulberry, Pineapple
11. Syconium : Fig
12. Efaerio of better : Annona sp
13. Ekaerro of Drupe lets : Strawberry

Commercial Method of Propagation: Fruits Method

1. Mango : Venner Grafiting
2. Banana : Sword suckers
3. Citrus : 'T'/ shield budding
4. Grapes : Hard wood cutting
5. Guar : Stooling/ Mound layering
6. Litchi. Programme to : Air Layering
7. Acid lime, Phalsa, Mangosrein : Seed
8. Apple, Pear, Peach, Plum : 'T' budding
9. Anola : Patch budding
10. Strawberry : Runner
11. Pineapples : sucker, slips

Nutrients, Deficiency symptoms and Sources:

Type	Deficiency	Source
Vitamin-a (Retinal)	Night blindness (xerophthalmia)	Fruits: Mango, Papaya, Japanese, Persimmon
Vit B-1 (Thiamin)	Beri-beri	Almond, Apricot, Cashew
Vit B-2 (Riboflavin)	Dry Skin	Bael, Passion Fruit, Jack
Vit C (Ascorbic acid)	Survey	F: Barbados Cherry, Orange, Guava, V: Chitlies, Bittergourd Amla
Vit – D (Calciferol)	Rickets	V: Greens
Iron	-	Dates, Currants, Caronda, Green
Calcium	-	Litchi, Banana, Carols, Tomato
Potassium	-	Banana, Greens
Phosphorus	-	Carrot, Tomato, Spinack
Iodine	Goatee	Onion Okra

CHAPTER THREE

BIOCHEMISTRY

Major group of compounds found in a cell are carbohydrates and their derivatives, fats and their derivatives proteins and their derivatives, nucleic acids.

1. CARBOHYDRATES

- Organic compounds with a general formula $(CH_2O)_n$
- Carbohydrates can be classified into 3 categories,

Monosaccharides
Oligosaccharides
Polysaccharides

a. Monosaccharides

- **Trioses:** Trioses are simple sugars derived from hydrolysis of oligopolysaccharides have 'C' atom ranging from 3-9 (eg.)
- They are of two types (a) Aldoses, (b) Ketoses
- **Aldoses:** Sugars with terminal CHO aldehyde group aldotriose- Glyceraldehyde (simplest sugar)

  - Aldoterose- Erythrose, thresose
  - Aldopentose – Arabiose ribose deoxyribose
  - Aldohexose – Glucose, galactose, mannose

- **Ketoses:** Having >C=O group
- **Ketotriose:** Dihydroxy acetone – simplest keto sugar
- **Ketohexose:** Fructose – It is the sweetest among all the sugars.

b. Oligosaccharides

- All derived from combination of two or more monosaccharides units Depending upon the number of monosaccharides presence they can be classified as

I.   **Disaccharides:** eg. Sucrose, Maltose, Lactose, cellobiose
II. **Trisaccharides:** eg. Raffinose
III. **Teirasaccharides:** eg. Stachyose

- **Sucrose:** Produced from alpha glucose beta fructose by alpha. –1.2. glycosidic linkage. It is a Non- reducing sugar.
- **Maltose:** Consists of 2 units of glucose linked together by alpha 1.4 linkage reducing sugar found in germinating seeds largely.
- **Cellobiose:** Consists of 2 units of glucose but the bond involved is beta, 1.4 linkage. It is a reducing sugar.
- **Lactose:** Consists of one molecule of beta D glucose and one molecule of beta D galactose linked together by beta 1.4 linkages.
- **Stachyose:** It is a tetra saccharide consists of one glucose and one fructose and 2 galactose.

A. Polysaccharides

- Molecular weight in kilo Daltons (kd)

a. Storage polysaccharides:

- In plant consists of amylase, amylopectin. (It is polymer of glucose).
- **Amylase** is un-branched chains of glucose units joined by alpha – 1.4 linkages. The chain is nonlinear, but it is helical one.
- **Amylopectin:** Highly branched, Bond types: Alpha-1.4 linkage but at the branching points alpha 1.6 linkage is present.
- **Glycogen:** It is present only in animal cells. It is just like starch, but heavily branched and compact and it contains both alpha 1.4 and alpha 1.6 linkages.

b. Structural Polysaccharides

- **Cellulose:** Polymer of glucose joined together by beta 1.4 linkage

- **Hemicellulose:** Polymer consisting of L-arabinose. D-glucose, D-galactose, D- Xylose, along with uranic acid (galacturonic acids)
- **Pectin:** Polymer of galacturonic acid. Normally present in cell walls as calcium Pectate

1. *PROTEINS*

- The name was suggested by Berzelius
- This name is derived from Greek Proteins means 'first rank'
- Proteins are polymer of amino acids.
- Each amino acid is linked with another one by peptide

$$-C=O-NH_2 \text{ bond.}$$

- Different structural levels:
- Primary structure- it is the linear arrangement of amino acids.

- Secondary structure- It is the structure found by linear Polypeptide chain which folds in a regular fashion.
- This may be of two kinds (1) alpha helix (2) beta pleated sheet.
- These secondary structures are produced by interaction between neighboring amino acids of same chain.
- Quaternary structure:
- The structure produced by association of more than one polypeptide
- Examples for some commonly occurring proteins
- Structural proteins :

  - Collagen: Muscle protein
  - Keratin: In hair and wool and nail
  - Fibroin: In silk
  - Elastin: Found in insect wings
  - Regulatory proteins : Enzymes
  - Transport proteins : Myoglobin, Haemoglobins

- Another classification of proteins:
- Simple proteins – Contains only ordinary amino acids
- Conjugated proteins – Proteins that contain non amino acid
- Components in addition to amino acids these additional factors are called prosthetic groups.
- Examples:

  - Nucleic proteins – Nucleic acid and protein – chromosomes
  - Glycoprotein – Protein and sugar units
  - Lipoproteins –Protein and lipids
  - Metalloproteins - metals and proteins haemoglobin

2. *ENZYMES*

- These are special classes of proteins. Enzymatic activity was first discovered by BUCHNER (Zymase was the first found initially from Yeast)
- The term enzyme was coined by W. KUHNS
- Terminology's Holoenzymes – Apoenzyme + Prosthetic group
- Apo-enzyme =Without prosthetic group
- Legend = Any substrata that binds with an enzyme
- Active site = The site responsible for analytic molecule
- Regulatory site = the site other than catalytic use where the regulatory.
- Characteristics of an enzyme:

- Specific, Protinacious, colloidal nature, sensitive to temperature.
- Enzymes do not change the equilibrium level. But quickens it.
- Mechanism of action of enzymes:

- It lowers down the activation energy.
- The lock and key model was proposed by Fisher
- Some special classes of enzymes.
- **Allosteric enzymes:** are regulatory enzymes which have more than one polypeptide

  - This type of enzymes have a well developed regulatory mechanism
  - They produce a sigmoidal curve (instead of classical parabolic curve)

- **Isozymes:** They are different enzymes which catalyze the same reaction in different tissues. They are different in molecular weight and exercised from different genes.
- **Ribozymes:** They are catalytic RNA with enzymatic property (non protein)
- Factors affecting activity of enzymes are Temperature. PH. Ionic strength. Water content.

1. *VITAMINS*

    - The term vitamins was introduced by FUNK
    - Classification:

2. Water soluble: – Vit. B complex (B_1, B_2, B_{12}) C
3. Niacin: (nicotinic acid)
4. Fat soluble: Vit: A. D. E. K.

    - **Vitamins** and their **deficiency symptoms**

    Vitamins Deficiency symptoms
    A (Retinal) :Xerophthalmia or dry Deonatosis (dry scaly skin)
    ,Night: blindness because of reduction in red cone cells
    B1 (thiamine) :BERI-BERI (Extreme weakness, pain in joints)
    B2 (Riboflavin) :Ariboflavinosis (Blurred vision, cracks on skin

at

    angle of mouth)
    B12 (Cyanocobalamin) :Pemiocin anemia (Reduction in RBCs)
B_6 NIACIN (Nicotinic :Pellagra (Black Tongue)
    acid (Peridoxin)
    C (Ascorbic acid) :Scurvy
    D (Calciferol) :Rickets (Pigeon chest in children), Osteomalacia
(adults)
    E (Alpha Tocopherol) :Sterility

    - Vitamins mainly act as **"cofactors"** for enzymatic activity.

4. *NUCLEIC ACIDS*

    - CLASSES DNA – Deoxyribose
    - RNA – Ribose
    - Nucleoside = Sugar (Ribose/ Deoxyribose) + Nitrogenous base
    - Nucleotide = Nucleoside + phosphate group

- Types of Bases

  - Adenine
  - Thymine/ uracil (RNA)
  - Guanine
  - Cytosine

- Nucleic acid: Frederick Mischer: Waston & crick – B DNA 9right handed helix)
- Bacteriophages – single stranded DNA
- Non-genetic RNAS
- t-RNA- Transfers amino acids from cytoplasm to Ribosome m-RNA- 5% carries the message from genes (DNA) r- RNA – Ribosomal RNA- Part of Ribosome (work benches of protein synthesis.

CHAPTER FOUR

MICRO BIOLOGY

History

- **Anton van Leeuwenhoek** : invented the simple (single biconvex lens) in 1674, Discovered Bacteria/microbial world
- **Louis Pasteur** : Postulated the 'germ theory' of disease, Pasteurization
- **Spallanzani** : First to provide evidence that micro-organisms do not arise spontaneously in organic in fusions
- **Robert Hooke** : Discovered compound microscope
- **Robert Koch** : Koch postulates for test of disease
- **Alexander Fleming (1929)** : Discovered antibiotic 'penicillium'
- **Iwanowsky (1892)** : Discovered Virus working with an extract from tobacco plants infected with mosaic disease
- **Beijerinck (1898)** : Named 'virus' (infectious poison agent)
- **Brefeld** : Developed pure culture techniques for isolation of micro-organisms
- **Hesse** : First introduced agar as a solidifying agent in culture media
- **Petri** : Designed and developed glass dishes known today as petridishes
- **Edward Jenner** : Developed vaccine for Small pox
- ROBERT HOOK – used the word CELL
- ROBERT BROWN – used the word NUCLEUS
- M. SCHLEIDEN & SCHWANN – Cell Theory
- Haeckel proposed PROTISTA

- Whittaker 5 kingdom classification

1. Monera – Prokaryotes
2. Protista – Unicellular Eukaryotes
3. Plantae (Photo syn.) – Multicellular plants and higher algae.
4. Fungi (adsorption) – Multinucleate higher fungi.
5. Animalia (ingestion)

- BERGY's manual of systematic bacteriology – is the standard for taxonomy
- Eukaryotic: Protozoa, fungi
- Prokaryotic : Bacteria, actinomycetes, BGA
- SIZE (approx.):

  - Bacteria – 0.5-3.0 micro m
  - Fungi – 1.5-10 micro m
  - Protozoa – 2-200 micro m
  - Viruses – 100-600 nano in MLO –0.1-0.3 micro m
  - Algae – 0.1 micro m (BGA) to 'x' feet (higher algae)
  - First living cell – e800 million year ago.
  - First prokayotic cell – 1400 million years ago (achaean cra)

- Sterilization:

  - A Physical agent: High Temp. – dry heat; 180^0 C; 1.5 HOURS – 2 HOUR

    - Moist heat; 1520 min (121.6c)
    - 15 pounds / inch pressure

- Pasteurization (with milk)

  - Low temp High time 62.8c (30 min)
  - High temp Low time 71,7c (15 second)
  - L. T. – Microbistatic (-4 to –7c)

- ◦ H. T. Desiccation
- ◦ Osmotic Pressure
- ◦ Radiation U. V. (2650 A- Lambda)
- ◦ Gamma rays. (Co 60)
- ◦ X-rays (5000-1,30,000 rads)

- ◦ Chemical agents

1. Phenol compound – cell wall; cyto. Membrane: protein denaturation
2. Alcohol's – Protein, cytoplasmic membrane
3. Iodine, chlorine, - Enzyme destruction. Amino acids
4. Aldehyde- amino acids + enzymes
5. Ethylene oxide (Gas) – Enzyme + Amino acids

Chemotheraputic agents:

1. Arsenic- for Syphilis (by Ehrlich)
2. Sulfonamide – for bacterial infection (by Domagk)

Antibiotics:-

- ◦ Penicillin – *Penicillium* sp – G + ve; cellwall synthesis
- ◦ Tetracycline - *S. aureofacines* – G + ve, G-ve; Protein synthesis
- ◦ Bacitracin – Bacillus subtilis – G + ve, cell wall synthesis
- ◦ Chloramphenicol – S. *venezuelae* G + ve; G-ve, Protein synthesis
- ◦ Cycloheximide – S. *venezuelae*, protein synthesis, Eukaryote
- ◦ Nystain – S. *nouresii* Eukaryote membrane
- ◦ Erythromycin – S. *nouresii* – fungi – Prokaryote
- ◦ Erythromyci – S. *erythreus* G + ve, G-ve, Protein synthesis
- ◦ Neomycin – S. *fradiae* G + ve, G-ve, protein synthesis

- • **Non legumes** – *Alnus, casurna, Myrica* – *Frankia*
- • **Associative Symbiosis** – *Azpospirillum*
- • **Symbiosis** – *Rhizobium*

- **Stem and root nodules** – Sesbania, *Azorbizobium caulonodans,*
- *Azospirillum and Azotobacter-* Cereals, oil seeds, vegetables, horticulture

- Seed treatment : 200g/ 1012 kg seeds
- Seedling treatment : 12 kg/ ha
- Setts treatment : 23 kg/q
- Soil treatment : 45 kg/ha

- Microscopy:

1. **Dark field microscope:**

   - Specimens are unstained, appear bright in a dark background
   - Applications- For gross morphology in the living specimen

2. Phase contrast microscope:

   - Unstained live microbial cells can be studied through this microscope
   - Applications – For revealing cellular structures in living cells
   - Enables to view living cells more clearly
   - Causes a slight loss of resolution

3. Bright field:

   - Specimen is stained or unstained
   - Used for studying gross morphology of yeasts, molds, algae etc.

4. U V microscope:

   - Appearance of specimen – Fluorescent
   - **Application** – For differentiating cellular components

5. Fluorescence microscopy:

   - Used for detecting specific types of antigens using an antibody tagged with fluorescent dye

6. Electron microscope:

   - Uses electromagnetic lenses and an electron beam
   - Resolving power and magnification is much higher than any light microscope
   - Viewed on fluorescent screen

7. Transmission electron microscope:

   - Contrast results from differential scattering of electrons by the specimen
   - Staining is done with salts of heavy metals as uranium. Tungsten

8. Scanning electron microscope:

   - Provide three dimensional image of the object
   - The surface topography of a specimen can be determined with a clarity and depth which is not possible by any other method

The Nitrogen Cycle:

- Nitrogen constitutes about 78% of the earth's atmosphere
- The nitrate form of nitrogen is mostly used by plants

a. Nitrification

   - Process of conversion of ammonia into nitrate

- Examples – **Nitrosomonas**(ammonia to nitrite), **Nitrobacteria**(nitrite to nitrate), *Aspergillus, Penicillium*

b. Denitrification

- Reduction of nitrate to nitrogen gas or nitrous oxide
- Occurs in waterlogged anaerobic soils
- Examples – *Thiobacillus, Pseudomonas*

Biological Nitrogen Fixation:

- Fixation of the inert atmospheric elemental nitrogen by micro-organisms through a reductive process
- Accounts for about **70%** of the total nitrogen fixed in the biosphere
- Restricted to **Bacteria only**

a. A symbiotic / Free living Nitrogen fixation:

- Aerobic – **Azotobacter**, **Blue green algae** (BGA)
- Anaerobic – ***Clostridium, Chlorobium, Rhodospirillum*** etc.

b. Symbiotic Nitrogen fixation:

- Example – ***Rhizobium, Bacillus*** etc.

Important points:

- Nitrogen fixing enzyme – **Nitrogenase** (First discovered in 1960 from *Clostridium pasteurianum*)
- Nitrogen fixing gene – **Nif genes**
- Elements involved in nitrogen fixation – **Molybdenum**
- Co-factor needed for nitrogen fixation – **Cobalt (Co)**
- Non legumes – **Alnus, Casuarina, Myrica, Frankia sp**
- Stem and root nodules – **Sesbania,** *Azorhizobium cauloncians*

- Leguminous crop not fixing nitrogen – **Rajma (*Phaseolus vulgaris)***
- *Phosphorus cycle – Bacillus, Pseudomonas, Micrococcus, Flavobacterium, Aspergillus, Penicillium, Fusarium*
- Sulphur cycle – Thiobacillus, Arthrobacter, *Desulfovibrio desulfuricans*
- Red pigment in the root nodules is known as **Leg haemoglobin**
- Bacteria not responsible for N-fixation- E.coli
- Nif gene is associated with – *Rhizobium bacteriod*
- Nitrogen fixation in rice field occurs due to presence of – Anabaena (BGA)

CHAPTER FIVE

CROP PHYSIOLOGY

RESPIRATION

- Respiration in plants consists of Glycolysis & Krebs Cycle and ETC (Electron Transport Chain)
- Glycolysis occurs in the cytoplasm & Krebs cycle and ETC in the mitochondria
- Glycolysis is anaerobic.
- Total ATP synthesis from on molecule of glucose in respiration is 36 ATP (Net gain) Gross production is 38 ATP
- Total ATP synthesis in glycolysis is 4 / glucose (Net gain – 2 ATP)
- Krebs cycle is also called as citric acid cycle or TCA (tricarboxylic acid cycle)
- Final product of glycolysis is pyruyate.
- Anaerobic respiration pathway products are ethanol and lactic acid.
- CO_2 molecules are released from the mitochondria during respiration.
- Krebs cycle starts with acetyl coA and oxaloacetate
- Election transport chain is present in the cristae of mitochondria where: ATP is synthesized in respiration.
- The high energy compound synthesized during respiration is by oxidative phosphorylation of ADP with P (inorganic

phosphate)

- Cytochromes are electron carriers involved in the respiratory election transport chain
- Energy content of molecule of glucose is 686 KCAL or 2870 KJ
- 1 molecule of ATP = 7.6 KCAL
- 1 molecule of NADH2 = 52 KCAL
- The energy currency of the cell is ATP
- Occurs in all living organisms except virus
- Catabolic process and oxidation-reduction reaction
- Raw materials used are glucose and oxygen
- During the breakdown of glucose molecule, 38 ATP molecules are formed
- Respiratory Quotient – ratio of Co_2 evolved to ratio of O_2 evolved, normal in plants – 0.97-1.17
- 36 ATP molecules are formed on complete oxidation of a glucose molecule through hexose monophosphate shunt cycle
- The net gain of energy by anaerobic respiration is 2 ATP molecules
- 1 molecule of ATP = 7.6 KCAL
- 1 molecule of $NADH_2$ = 52 KCAL
- The no of Co2 molecule released between anaerobic and aerobic respiration is zero
- The ratio of energy released between anaerobic and aerobic respiration is 1:18

b. Glycolysis:

- Called as EMP pathway (Embden Meyerof paranas pathway) refers to degradation of glucose to two pyruvic acid molecules
- Occurs in cytosol of cytoplasm
- Common for aerobic and aerobic respiration
- Pyruvic acid is the end product of Glycolysis
- Total ATP synthesis in Glycolysis is 4 glucose (Net gain – 2 ATP)

b. Krebs cycle:

- Also called TCA cycle, citric acid cycle, organic acid cycle, mitochondrial respiration
- The first stable product is citric
- Kreb's cycle occurs in matrix of mitochondria-aerobic condition
- Krebs cycle starts with acetyl COA and oxaloacetate
- In Krebs cycle, the mineral activator required for enzyme aconitase is Fe

- The only 5 C compound in TCA cycle is α- Ketoglutaric acid

c. Electron transport chain:

- Also called as respiratory chain or oxidative phosphorylation
- In general, it is found inside the mitochondria
- The process occurs on the inner membrane of cristae

PHOTOSYNTHESIS

- Total carbon fixed by land per year = 110×10^{12}
- Total carbon fixed by ocean per year = 273×10^{11}
- Blackmann – Explained the law of limiting factors
- Calvin (1954) – Traced the path of carbon in photosynthesis and gave the C_3 cycle
- Hatch and Slack (1965) – Reported C_3 pathway for carbon dioxide fixation in certain tropical grasses
- The reduction of Co2 to carbohydrate level needs assimilatory products such as ATP and $NADPH + H^+$
- Reduction of Co2 occurs in dark but the production of assimilatory powers is light dependent
- Major photosynthetic pigments of higher plants are Chlorophyll a and Chlorophyll b
- Important accessory pigments in plants are carotenoids and xanthophylls

- Light reaction of photosynthesis takes place in thylakoids or Grana
- Dark reaction of photosynthesis take place in stroma
- Photosynthesis is an oxidation-reduction process

a. Calvin cycle (C_3 plants):

- The Co_2 acceptor is Ribulose 1, 5- diphosphate
- The first stable product of photosynthesis is a 3 carbon compound Phosphoglyceric acid (PGA)
- For synthesis of one glucose molecule 18 ATP are required
- Photorespiration is present and easily detectable
- Bundle sheaths cells are unspecialised
- The enzyme RUBP carboxylase or Rubisco is found in chloroplast stroma and is the most abundant protein on earth
- Examples of C_3 plants – Wheat, Barley, Oat, Rye, Rice, Pea, Soybean

b. Hatch and slack cycle (C_4 PLANTS):

- The Co_2 acceptor is phosphoenolpyruvic acid (PEP)
- Oxaloacetic acid (oxaloacetate) is the first stable product
- Photorespiration is present only to a slight degree or absent
- 30 ATP are required for the synthesis of one glucose molecule
- The most distinguishable anatomical feature of the leaves of C4 plants is the presence of bundle sheath cells containing chloroplasts
- The bundle sheath cells lack Grana in their chloroplast
- Leaves of C_4 plants show Kranz type of anatomy
- PEPCO enzymes are present in C_4 plants
- C_4 cycle is found only in certain tropical plants
- C_4 plants are about twice as efficient as C_3 plants in converting solar energy into the production of dry matter
- Example of C_4 plants – sugarcane, maize, pearl millet, *Cyperus rotundus* etc.

c.   Crassulacean acid metabolism cycle (CAM cycle):

- Occurs in mesophyll cells
- Most (not all) CAM plants possess the succulent habit
- Examples – Bryophyllum, Opuntia, Agave, Pineapple etc.
- Total carbon fixed by land per year = 110 x1012

- Total carbon fixed by ocean per year = 273 x 1011
- Photosynthesis active radiation (PAR) = 400to 700 nm
- Major photosynthetic pigments of higher plants are Chlorophyll a & chlorophyll b
- Important accessory pigments is plants are carotenoids – (1) caroteins, (2) xanthophylls
- Co2 concentration in the atmosphere is 350 ppm
- Photosynthesis reaction : $Co2 + 2H2o + light = C_6 H_{12} O_6 + H2O + O2$
- Two parts of photosynthesis:
- Light it action or hill reaction takes place in grana of chloroplast dark reaction of Calvin
- Cycle takes place in stroma of chloroplast
- The products of the light reaction are ATP and NADPH2

Three types of Photosynthesis Mechanisms

- C_3 pathway or reductive pentose pathway or Blackman reaction (Calvin cycle): Rice, Wheat, Pea, Soyabean, Barley.
- C_4 pathway (Hatch – sack pathway or Dicarboxylic acid pathway): Sorghum, Maize, Sugarcane or B-carboxylation cycle or cooperative Photo synthesis
- CAM pathway (Crassulacean acid metabolism) (Pineapple, opuntia, Agave)
- The most important enzyme involved in photosynthetic CO_2 fixation is Rubisco (Ribulose-bi phosphate carboxylase).
- Rubisco is also the most abundant protein in the world.
- C_3 plant first enzyme in CO_2 fixation: Rubisco

- C_4 Plants first enzyme in CO_2 fixation: PEP carboxylase
- Water use efficiency: CAM>C_4>C_3
- In photosynthesis light energy is converted into chemical energy
- Light reaction takes place in the Thylakojds and dark reaction takes place in the stroma of
- the chloroplast
- Higher productive plants: C_4 (Maize, S. Cane, sorghum)
- High productive plants: C_3 (Wheat, Rice Pulses)
- Low Productive plants: CAM (Pineapple)
- C4 plants two types of photosynthesis cells; Mesophyll cells and bundle sheath cells (Kranz type leaf anatomy)
- Photorespiration occurs in C3 plants in light only.
- Normal respiration/ Dark respiration occurs in all cells all the time in all the plants.
- Calvin cycle & Hatch – Slack pathway occurs in chloroplast
- Chlorophyll molecule contains Mg^3+ion in its structure
- Photosynthetic rate is the highest in C_4 plants
- The processes of formation of ATP in chloroplast with the help of light is called as
- photophosrylation or photosynthetic phosporylation.
- First product of photosynthesis – 3 PGA in C3
- One NADH2 will prpoduce 3 ATP
- One FADH2 will produce 2 ATP

PHOTORESPIRATION

- Refers to production of Co_2 in respiration from 2 C compounds in presence of light
- Reported only in green cells such as *Beta, Phaseolus, glycine, Oryzae, Pisum, Gossypium, Capsicum, Helianthus* etc
- Discovered by DECKER in tobacco plants
- Substrate for photorespiration is glycolic acid (2 c) and hence called as C2 cycle or glycolate metabolism

- It occurs in between chloroplast, cytosol, peroxisome and mitochondria

- It occurs in C_3 plants and temperate plants
- The presence of photorespiration process decreases the photosynthetic efficiency of plants
- Photorespiration is said to be highest in Rice
- Serine amino acid is produced in photorespiration
- Photorespiration involves more than one organelle
- In photorespiration, NAD is reduced to $NADH_2$

MINERAL NUTRITION

- Essential element – (criteria proposed by Arnon and stout)

1. In the absence of that element, plants is not able to complete its life cycle
2. The element should not be substituted by other element
3. Element should form a part of any molecule or constituent of the plant.

- Beneficial element –They do not form the constituent of plant can grow without it but if present it is advantageous to the plant
- Macronutrients: C, H, O, N, S, Ca, Mg, K, P (>100 µg/g dry matter)
- Micronutrients : Cl, Fe, B, Mn, Zn, Cu, Mo (100 µg/ g dry mater)
- Mobile elements: N,P,K, Mg, Mn, Mo, Cl, Zn and Na
- Immobile elements: Bo, Fe, Ca, Cu, S
- Beneficial elements: Co, Sl, Selenium, Na, Ni
- Cobalt: Legumes
- Silicon: Rice, Maize
- Nickel: Legumes

- Criteria of the essentiality of mineral elements propose by Arnon and stout
- Atleast 60 elements are present in plants out of which only 16 are essential
- **Carbon:** (46% dry weight basis)

  - **Source:** Co2 from the air
  - **Function:** Most of the compounds in the living cells are C-containing.

- **Oxygen:** (50%)

  - **Source:** O2, Co2, H2o
  - **Function:** The most abundain elements by weight in plants Required for all compounds in plants.

- **Hydrogen:** (6%)

  - **Source:** H_2O
  - **Function:** Most abundant elements by number of atoms Present in all the compounds in the living cell component of H_2O

- **Nitrogen:** 1.5%

  - **Source:** NO3, NH4 in the soil solution, Legumes through N2 fixation.
  - **Function:** All the crops prefer No3-(Nitrate) except Rice which prefers NH4 + (ammonium)
  - **Components** of nucleic acid. Chlorophyll molecule, Proteins
  - **Deficiency:** Pale yellow leaves & reduced growth redleaves in cereals
  - Red colour develops in Apple due to the anthocyanin production

- ◦ Root lengthening in wheat
- ◦ Excess Nitrogen leads to vegetative growth, delay in flowering

- **Phosphorus:** (0.2-0.8%)

  - ◦ **Source** : H3PO4 & Hpo4 from the soil solution
  - ◦ **Function**: Component of nucleic acid, Phospholipids (Membranes), ATP
  - ◦ **Deficiency**: variable colour development in leaves (Dark green) reduced tillering & leaf fall. Anthocyanin produced give pink colour.

- Potassium:

  - ◦ Only present in plants as K+ not bound to any components
  - ◦ **Function**: Stomatal closing & opening
  - ◦ Disease resistance
  - ◦ Osmotic adjustment, needed for cell elongation
  - ◦ **Deficiency**: rosette, die back in plants

- Chlorosis:

  - ◦ Stunted growth & Thin shoots
  - ◦ Tip burns & leaf scorch in older leaves

- Magnesium

  - ◦ Constitutent of chlorophyll
  - ◦ Activates many enzymes
  - ◦ **Deficiency**: Older leaves affected Cholorosis. Sand drown disease in tobacco

- **Sulphur:** 0.1%

- ○ **Source**: Soluble sulphates
- ○ **Functions**: Aminoacids (Cystein and Methonene)
- ○ Coenzyme A
- ○ Volatile Oils
- ○ **Deficiency**: Downward cupping of leaves e.g. tobacco, Torr, Tea,
- ○ Tea yellow disease
- ○ Chlorosis

- Calcium:

  - ○ **Functions**: Calcium pectate is present in the middle lamella of the cell wall
  - ○ ATPase activator
  - ○ Counteract metal toxicity
  - ○ **Deficiency**: Young leaves are mostly affected
  - ○ Hooked tips & distort leaves

- Iron

  - ○ Component of cytochromes, Catalase, peroxidase
  - ○ Deficiency: L
  - ○ Intervienal Chlorosis (iron Chlorosis)
  - ○ Leaf bleaching (S. Cane)

Deficiency symptoms of Elements:

- N: general starvation
- Fe: Intervienal chlorosis e.g. S. Cane
- Mn: Grey speck Disease of oats, pahla blight of sugarcane, marsh spot of pea
- Copper: Die back disease of citrus or exanthema, Reclamation, white tip disease
- Zinc: Mottled leaf of citrus, drenching of citrus

- Little leaf/ Rosette as in Apple, Pine, Peach walnut, citrus etc, white tip of maize
- Khaira disease of rice
- Molybdenum: Whip tail of cauliflower and brassicae, scald of legumes
- Boron: Heart rot of sugar beet and marigold
- Canker of table beet
- Browning & Hallow stem of cauliflower
- Cracked stem of alfa-alfa
- Hard fruits of Citrus
- Top sickness of Tobacco
- Water core of turnip
- Phosphorus: Sickle leaf disease
- Calcium: blossom End Rot (BER) in tomato and Tip hooking in cauliflower

PLANT GROWTH REGULATORS:

- **Thiamann** – suggested the use of term "Phytohormone" in plants
- Phytohormone are organic substances which are naturally produced in plants

AUXINS (weakly acidic growth hormone):

- Auxin was named by KOGL. It is a Greek word derived from 'Auxein' which means to grow
- Naturally occurring Auxin – IAA
- Synthetically produced auxins are – NAA, IBA, 2, 4 – D, MCPA
- Anti-auxins – Naphthythalamic acid (NTA) , Ethylene chlorohydrins
- Active sites of auxins – shoot tip region, coleoptiles and developing embryos etc.

- The Auxin synthesis occurs rapidly in green leaves in presence of light than the in the dark
- Tryptophan is the precursor of IAA and zinc is required for its synthesis
- Translocation of auxins is polar
- The site of Auxin transport is located on the plasma lemma
- Avena curvature test and split pea stem curvature test are the bioassays that are generally used for auxins
- Role of auxins:

1. Promotes apical dominance
2. Increases cell division in cambium
3. Promote the elongation of cells
4. Auxin increase in shoot and decrease in root
5. Induces uniform flowering in pineapple
6. IBA promotes rooting of cutting

GIBBERELLINS:

- Second important growth hormone found in plants
- Discovered by KUROSAWA (1926)
- First isolated from *Gibberella fujikuroi*, the causal organism of "foolish seedling of rice" or commonly called Bakanae disease of rice.
- Gibberellins are CYCLIC DITERPENES with gibbane skeleton
- Gibberellins moves in both xylem and phloem
- Chemically gibberellins are related to terpenoids and its precursor is N- Kaurene
- Anti- gibberellins: phosphon D, Cycocel (CCC), Maleic hydrazide, paclobutrazol
- Role of gibberellins:

1. Breaking of dormancy
2. Induction of flowering in long day plants

3. Promotes male flowers production
4. Enhances seed germination
5. The most important effect of GA is the stem elongation i.e. GA induces internode elongation or sub apical elongation

CYTOKININS:

- Plays a key role in higher plants and moves through xylem
- Miller and Skoog – identified kinetin
- Term cytokinin proposed by Letham (1963)
- The first naturally occurring hormone identified – Zeatin
- Root tip is an important site of cytokinin synthesis
- Precursor of cytokinin is either **adenine or adenosine** i.e. purine bases
- Mobility is polar and basipetal
- Role of cytokinin:

1. Initiation of cell division
2. Delay of senescence
3. Induce flowering in short day plants

4. Promotes stomatal opening
5. Promote femaleness in male flowers

ABSCISSIC ACID (ABA):

- Naturally occurring growth regulator
- It acts as stress hormone
- ABA first identified by WAREING (1965)
- Lunalaric acid found in algae and liverworts acts similar to abscissic acid
- Violoxanthin serves as a precursor for biosynthesis of ABA
- Biosynthesis of ABA also takes place through mevalonic acid
- It is a terpenoids

- Bioassays are – rice seedling growth inhibition test and inhibition of α amylase in

barley endosperm

- Role of ABA:

1. Induces bud dormancy and enhances the process of abscission
2. Senescence of leaf is promoted by ABA
3. Stimulates the release of ethylene
4. Brings the closure of stomata during water stress
5. ABA is called ANTI- GIBBERELLIN.

ETHYLENE:

- It is known as **RIPENING HORMONE**
- Production increased with increase in respiration rate
- Auxin increases ethylene level in plants
- Naturally occurring volatile hormone
- BURG (1962) established that ethylene is the only gaseous growth regulator
- Maximum ethylene is formed in ripening fruits and senescing tissues
- Biosynthesis of ethylene occurs from methionine which is a sulphur containing amino acid
- Inhibitors of ethylene synthesis are amino-ethoxyvinylglcine
- Bioassays for ethylene are triple pea test and pea stem swelling test
- Role of ethylene:

1. Responsible for fruit ripening with increase in respiration
2. Induces uniform flowering and ripening in pineapple
3. Inhibits stem elongation and cause abscission of leaves
4. Induces fruiting in ornamental plants
5. ETHEPHON- increase latex flow in rubber

OTHERS:

- **Glysophosine** – used to ripen sugarcane
- **Florigen (flowering hormone)** – initiation of flowering in plants
- **Traumatic acid (wound hormone)** – found in injured portions of a plant
- **Xanthoxin** – destruction product of Violoxanthin and forms ABA
- **Brassins** – steroid, isolated from pollen grains of Brassica
- **Jasmonic acid** – Methyl ester in jasmine, inhibits growth and promote senescence

Important points:

- Potassium ions (K^+) play an important role in the opening and closing of stomata
- Plant transpirants – colourless plastics, silicone ols, phenyl mercuric acetate, Absiccic acid, Co_2 etc.
- Porometer is used for measuring transpiration
- The growth is maximum during exponential phase
- Transpiration takes place through stomata, lenticels or cuticle
- Guttation refers to exudation of water from plants in the form of liquids

- **Short day plants** – soybean, potato, sugarcane, cosmos, chrysanthemum, tobacco, rice, onion, upland cotton, strawberry, datura etc
- **Long day plants** – spinach, lettuce, radish, alfalfa, sugar beet, opium, poppy, oats, wheat etc.
- **Day neutral plants** –tomato, cucumber, cotton, pea, sunflower, maize etc.
- **Vernalisation** – refers to method on inducing early flowering in plants by pre- treatment of their seeds at very low

temperature
- Hormone responsible for vernalisation is vernalin
- Water use efficiency is highest in CAM plants followed by C_4 and C_3 plants
- Photosynthetic efficiency is highest in C_4 plants
- To make one molecule of glucose, 6 turns of Calvin cycle are required
- The efficiency of photosynthesis is 40 %
- The ratio of photosynthesis to respiration during day time is 10:1
- In most succulent plants, Co_2 is fixed by the activity of PEP carboxylase
- The ratio of Co_2 reduced and oxygen released during photosynthesis is 1:1
- DCMU is an example of photosynthetic inhibitor
- The products of light reaction are ATP and NADPH2
- Major form of carbon transfer in plants is by sucrose
- For photosynthesis, the visible range of spectrum between 250 to 750 nm is essential

CHAPTER SIX

ENTOMOLOGY

PESTS OF SUGARCANE

1. **Shoot borer:** *Chilo infuscatellus* (crambidae) or early shoot borer

    - Number of feeding punctures near the base of shoot. Rotten portion of straw colored dead heart emits offensive odour. It can be pulled out eastly.
    - **Control:** Earthing up during early stage.

        - Trash mulching
        - Trichogramma Chilonis

    - Soil application of Gammas HCH emulsion @ 1 kg a.i./ha over the cane sets in famous at the time of planting
    - Granulosis Virus can also be used

2. **Top borer:** Scirphophaga excerptalis (Pryalidae)

    - Midrib tunnelling. Shot – holes on axial bud growth leaves, dead heart and can be pulled out easily and given bunchy top appearance, Acrial root formation.
    - **Control:**

i. Avoiding of frequent irrigation
ii. Carbofuran @ 1 kg a.i./ha synchronizing with brood emergence

iii. Trichogramma japonicum
iv. Pre-pupal parasitoid Isotima Javensis
v. Resistant var: COJ67, CO 1007

1. **Internode borer:** *Chilo sacchaviphagus indicus (crambidac)*

   - Attack starts from 4th months onwards. Internodes constricted and shortened with many bore holes: fresh bore holes with wet frass, stunted growth. Major pests in peninsular India. Hardening of internodes.
   - **Control:** Detrashing at 5.7 & 9th months

   -T- chilonis @ 3.5 cc/ha/fortnight from 4th month until a month before harvest.

4. **Gurdaspur borer:** (Crambidae) *Acigone steniellea*

   - Two phases: Gegarious phase – feed on first internode from to & may larvae enter into the core through single hole.
   - Solitary phase – dispersed to other came by silhen treads.

5. **White grub:** *Holotrichia consanguinea: H. Serrata. (Meloionthidae Anomula begglensis* (Rutelinae)

   - Drying of crops : Yellowing & nibbling of leaves: roots eaten away.
   - Control: *Netarhizium onisopliae*

     ◦ Pudding & crop rotation
     ◦ B. *Popillae* milky disease

6. **Termites:** *Odentotermes spp: Microtermes obesi*

   - Older leaves dry up first & cane falls down if disturbed.
   - Filled with moist soil inside the papery rind.

7. **Sugarcane scale:** *Melanaspis glomerate:* (diaspridiadae)

- Grayish block appearance of stem. Reduced yield, juice quality of Jaggery production
- Control: Detrashing & Trash burning.

8. **Leaf hopper:** *Pyrilla perpusilla* (Lophopidae)

- Yellowish white spots on leaves; sooty mould on later stages.
- Control: Externel parasitoid: *Epiricarlia melanoleuca* (Ephpyropidae)
- Green muscardine fungus: *Aceria sacchari* (Eriophyidae)
- Forming a circular Ereneum gall in the inner side of the leaf sheath

PESTS OF WHEAT

- The rabi crops which are seriously damaged by white grub beetle are wheat and potato.
- **Wheat shootfly**: *Atherigona naquii*
- **Ghujia weevil**: *Taenymecus indicus* is a pest of wheat, barley gram and mustard. The adult weevils cut to germinating seedlings grub feed on soil humus.
- **Wheat aphid**: *Macrosiphum miscanthi*
- **Wheat gall nematode** or **ear cockle nematode**: *Anguina triticl* Bacterium associated:

Corynebacterium tritici

- **Seed galls/ Thundu disease/ yellow ear rot** (Bacterium+Nematode)

o Mgt. Hot water treatment of seeds at 50^0C for 2 hrs.

- **Wheat stems borer:** *Sesamia inferens* (Noctuidae).

PESTS OF RICE

- **Yellow stem borer**: *Scirpophaga incertulas* (Pyraustidae)

  - Deed heat in young seedlings
  - White earhead in panicle stage. No grain formation.
  - Monophagous pest

Control:

- **Parasitiods**: *Tetrastichus Schoenobii*; egg parasitiod *Trichogramma Japonicum*

○ Destruction of stubbles
○ Host plant resistance: TKM 6 resistant variety contains *Penta deconal* & silica.
○ Pheromone Oviposition deterants in rice for stem borer

- **Gall fly or gall midge**: *Orseoeoa oryzae* (Cecidomyiidae)

○ Silver shoot or onion leaf which is a modified leaf sheathcaused by maggot.
○ Bio control agent: Playigaster oryzae

- **Leaf folder**: *cnapholocrocis medinalis* (Pyraustidae)

○ Longitadial folding of leaves & drying of leaves by larva.
○ Control: Avoid use of excess nitrogen
○ Parasitoids: *Trichogramma Japomcum*

- **Green leaf hopper**: *Nephotettix virescens* (Cicadellidae)

○ yellowing of leaves
○ Vector of rice Tungro, Yellow dwarf, Transitory yellowing

- **Brown planthopper:** Nilaparvata lugens (Delphacidae)

○ Hopper burn drying burning symptom in young plants. Circular patches of drying. Vector of grassy stunt. Ragged stunt and wilted stunt.
○ Avoid use of excess nitrogen
○ Resistant varieties: Py3, CO42, Mudgo (low aspargine content)
○ Resurgence causing pesticides: Acephate, Fenthion, Phosphamidon, synthetic Pyrethriods, Methyl demeton
○ Predators: *Cyrtorhimus lividipennis Lycosa sp. Microvetia* sp.

- **Ear head bug**: *Leptocorisa acuta:* L. *oratorius* (Gundhi bug) (Alydidae): chaffy grains with black spot. Feeds on tender stem. Peduncle and milky grains leads to chaffy ear head.

○ **Control**: Fenthion 100 EC 200 ml
○ Malathion 5% dust @ 10 kg/ha.
○ Clean cultivation- removal of weeds & grasses.

- **Rice root nematode:** *Hirschmaiviella oryzae* (Mentck disease)
- **White up rematode or spring dwarf nematode:** *Aphelexhcopdes besseyi* hot water treatment of seeds at 52^{0}C for to min.

- **Rice stem nematode:** *ditylenchus angustus*

- Larva disease in rice.

- **Rice case worm**: *Nymphula depunctalis*

- Larva with in tubular cases. Floating on water.

PESTS OF COTTON:

- consuming 54% of total inscticide in India though the area under cotton is only 5%

1. **Cotton jassid or leafhopper**: *Amrasca devastans (A.biguttula biguttula cicadellidae)*

   - Hopper burn yellowing, curling, bronzing & drying.

2. **Whitefly: *Bemisia tabaci* (Aleyrodidae)**

   - Shedding of leaves, stunting of plants, bud boll opening and poor quality lint., contamination of lint with honey dew and sooty mould appearance.
   - Vector of cotton leaf curl virus disease in Punjab.
   - Whitefly outbreak on cotton in AP during 1985-86.
   - Outbreak was due to indiscriminate use of insecticides particularly synthetic pyrethroids against Heliothis.

3. **Spotted bollworm**: *Earias vitella*

   - Spiny bollworm: *Earias insulana* (Noctuidae)
   - Symptom: Boring of terminal shoots of young, plants "Flaring of squares" and boring of young bolls frass at the entrance hole.
   - Moths are green in colour.

4. **Pink bollworm**: *Pectinophora gossypiella* (Gelichidae)

   - Symptom: Rosetting of flowers
   - Eating of seeds
   - Double seed formation, Locular burrowing
   - Diapause during winter

5. **American bollworm**: *Helicoverpa armigera* (Noctuidae)

- Large, circular bore holes with faecal pellets. Larvae feed by thrusting their heads alone inside.

6. **Red cotton bug:** *Dysdercus cingulatus* (Pyrrhocoridae)

- Roting of bolls: water soaked spots
- Lay eggs in soil
- Bacterim associated: *Nematospora gossypii* – staining of hint.
- Control measures: All pests
- Crop rotation with cereal: i) Bhendi should not be grown in rotation

  - ii) Yellow sticky trap for monitoring whitefly
  - iii) Whitefly tolerant var. LPS 141 and Supriya
  - iv) Pheromone trap for PBW (Gossyplure)

- Pheromone trap for Helicopiveria (Helilure)
- Biological control:

  - *Trichogramma chilonis* against bollworms
  - Spodoptera NPV 250-500 LE/ha (1 LE=6×10^9 POB= 3 larvae)
  - Helicoverpa NPV
  - B.t. Formulation against early instars of bollworms
  - Synthetic pyrethriods should be used only during peak flowering and boll formation stages.

7. **Stem weevil:** *Pempherulus affinis*

- Stem gall near the base of the plant
- MCU 3 – resistant variety
- Control – soil application of granular insecticide/Neem cake

PESTS OF CHICK PEA (BENGAL GRAM)

- *Helicoverpa armigera* – Gram pod borer or gram caterpillar consume foliage and developing pods.
- *Greasy cutworm, Agrotis ypsilon* (Noctuidae) Cut the stems at ground level

TERMINOLOGY:

- *Regular pest:* Occur most frequently on cultivated crops Eg.: cotton bollworms, Brinjal fruit borer
- *Occasional pest:* Occurring less frequently Eg.: case worm on rice
- **Seasonal pests:** Occurs in a particular season of year Eg.: red hairy caterpillar on groundnut
- **Persistent pest:** Occurs throughout the year on crops Eg.: chilli thrips, Rose thrips
- **Sporadic pests:** Occurs in a few isolated localities Eg.: Gall midge on rice in Madurai area
- **Endemic pests:** Occurs in same Agril. Area year after year Eg.: nematode on potato in Nilgris
- **Migratory pests:** Moves from one area to others and causes damage Eg.: Locust
- **Epidemic pests:** Occur in particular area/season in severe form
- **Pandemic pests:** Occur in a large geographical area/entire country or continent Eg.: locust outbreak

AGRONOMY

PRINCIPLES OF AGRONOMY:
CLIMATE AND ITS INFULENCE ON CROPS

- **Weather** is a condition of atmosphere at a given place at a given time
- **Climate** is a weather condition over a given region during a longest period.
- Structure of atmosphere
- Troposphere- statosphere- Mesosphere – Ionosphere par
- All weather phenomous like rain, fag, above mist occur in *Troposphere* zone found in stratosphere.
- **Solar constant:** Energy falling in one minute is a surface area of one square cm at the outer boundary of atmosphere.
- It is equivalent to 1.94 cal/cm^2 /min.
- Photosyntheticaly Active Radiation
- Photoperiodic effect – influence of crop growth by the relative length of day and night especially for floral inition
- Long day plant – plants require long day (>14 hrs.) for floral inifiation (eg. Wheat, Barley, Oat)
- Short day plant – Plants require shorkerday (less than 10 hrs) (eg. Rice, Sorghum Maize)
- Neutral plants – cotton, sunflower, buck wheat
- Average rainfall in India – (120 cm)
- Rain bearing clouds – cumulonimbus, cumulus.

- Rainy day – if the rainfall received is more than 2.5 mm on a particular day it is called as rainy day.
- *Instruments*

  - Radiation: Pyranometer: Pressure : Barograph
  - Photosynthetically active radition: quantum sensor
  - Temperature: Thermograph: Humidity-Psychrometer (or) hygrometer
  - Dew: Darosometer: water table: Pizometer rain –Raingauge
  - Soil moisture : Tensiometer

- Chemical used for cloud seeding – Silver iodide for cold clouds sodium chloride for warm cloud
- Indian Meteorological organization situated in PUNE
- Isotherm – Lines of equal temperature
- Isobar – Lines of equal pressure
- Isohyets- Lineo of equal rainfall
- Isotach – Lines of equal wind speed
- Kharif season crop- June to September crops (sorghum, maize, rice, cotton, pegion pea, other pulses, ground nut)
- Rabi season crops – crop grown during winter (October March) eg. wheat, chickpea, oat, barley, sun flower.

GROWTH AND DEVELOPMENT

- C_3 plant – eg. Rice, wheat , cotton, soybean
- Enzyme- ribulose 1.5-bisphosphate carboxylate photorespiration is high in C_3 plants (Rubisco)
- C_4 Plants- sugarcane, maize, sorgham pearl millet enzyme PEP Carboxylase
- CAM- Pine apple; sisal, ogave
- Plant growth regulators (commercial use) in Agriculture.
- **Abscisic acid**- Cotton defoliatant; 2.4, -D- herbicide
- **Glyphosate** – Sugarcane ripener: gabbroic acid – seed less grape
- NAA- fruits thinner, flower initiation

- MH – Succur control in tobacco, Ethelene – ripening of fruits

SOIL & FERTILIZER

- Soil fertility – Inherent capacity of soil to supply adequated nutrients
- Soil Productivity – Capacity of soil to produce in terms of yields.
- Soil texture – relative proportion of soil particles i.e. clay silt. And sand
- Soil structure – arrangement of soil particles
- Particle dimension: Sand 0.2 to 0.02, silt 0.02 to 0.002
- Clay < 0.002, gravel> 2mm
- Crumby structure is better for crop cultivation
- Pore space occupied by water and rain
- Total pore space is more in clay soil
- Bull density – weight of soil per unit volume- $1.5 g/cm^3$
- Particle density – weight of solid portion of soil per unit volume – $2.6 g/cm^3$
- % pore space – Particle density – bulkdensity x 100 particle density
- Soil air- Co2 concentration over 0.3%
- Well decomposed organic matter is called as humus
- Carbon: Nitrogen (C:N) ration for organic matter – 12:1

  - Legume – 23:1 cereals –90% FYM : 100

- Soil water:
- Field capacity – the soil moisture held by the soil against gravitation
- Force: energy status - -0.1 to 0.33 bar
- Available soil moisture: -0.33 bar to –15 bar =1569 g
- Annual fertilizer consumption: 16:18 MT
- Per ha fertilizer consumption = 76:8 kg/ha
- Fertilizer :

- Organic fertilizer – urea; Neutral fertilizer – CAN 9calcium ammonium nitrate)
- Recommended ratio of NPK for crops 4:2:1 NPK
- At present India to consumption ratio: 9:3:1 NPK
- Per area fertilizer consumption more in Punjab union feretory
- Pondichery. Total pesticide consumption
- Deficiency disorders:
- Mn. Gray speck in oat, Marsh spot in pea, pahala blight in sugarcane
- Cu. Reclamation disease in cereals
- Zn. Kharif in rice, white (bud) in maize, Frenching on citrus
- Mo. Whiptail is cauliflower
- Mg. Is a constituent of chlorophyll
- Bo. Browning of cauliflower
- Symbiotic nitrogen fixing bacteria: Rhizobium
- Gene responsible for N fixation – Nif genes
- Micro element needed for N fixation Molybdenum
- Free living N fixing bacteria *Azotobactor,* clostridium
- Micro organism associated with casuavina frankia
- Conversion of ammonia to nitrite – Nitrosomonas,
- Conversion of nitrite of Nitrate- Nitrobacter

TILLAGE

- Tilth physical condition of soil resulting from Tillage
- Implements used for primary tillage: country plough , Mouldboard, Plough, Bose plough
- Implements used for secondary tillage –(blade harrow, disc harrows tractor drawan ultivator)
- Breeding sub soil – chisel plough
- Pudding – Wet land puddler, tractor drawn cage wheel
- Sowing – Mechanical seed drill
- Weeding – Japanese rotary weeder
- Net sown = 143 mha (1998) and 142.22 mha 1999
- Rainfed = 92 mha (1998)

- Irrigated = 50 mha, 25 mha (37.6%)

IRRIGATION

- Potential area under irrigation 89.44 mha
- Major irrigation project – Project covering more than 10,000 ha of command area
- **Medium** – 2000- 10,000ha
- **Minor** irrigation project – less than 2000 ha
- 1 ha cm = 1 lakh liter of water 1 cubic metre – 1000 litre of water
- 1 cu feet – 28.32 liters
- Duty of water – Number of hectare irrigated by constant flow of one current of water
- Delta – Total depth of water irrigated by one ha.
- **Transpiration** – gaseous loss of water from the surface leaf
- **Evapotranspiration** – Evaporation + Transpiration
- **Water use efficiency** – Ratio between yield and Evapotranspiration or WUE = Y/ ET
- Consumptive use
- Irrigation efficiency more in clay soil. less the sandy soil
- Type of irrigation
- **Flooding** – rice, check basins wheat finger millo (ground pit)
- **Basin method** – Fruit, crops: furrow irrigation, cotton, sugarcane tobacco, vegetables; sprinkler undulated areas

DRY FARMING

- The practice of crop production entirely with rainwater received during the crop season in low rainfall (<800mm) areas is called as dry or dryland farming.
- **Arid climate**: Extremely dry climate with an annual average precipitation usually less than 250 mm.
- **Seed hardening**: Process of subjecting seeds before sowing to alternate cycle of wetting and drying to induce tolerance to drought.

- **Proline:** Chemicals, K2H2SO4, KCL 0.5 is an amino acid which is increased in plants during drought.
- **Water harvesting** – Collecting and storage water on the surface of soil for subsequent use.
- **Antitrans pirants** – Any material applied to transpiring plant surfaces for reducing water loss.
- Types:

  - Stomatal closing type- Phenyl mercuric acetate (PMA)
  - Film forming type – Mobileaf, Silicone oil
  - Reflectant- Kaoline spray
  - Growth retartent – cycocel

HERBICIDES

- Selective herbicide – Kills only targeted plants on weeds while crops are ont affected Eg. Siomazine, atrazine, 2,4-D butachlor, alachlor, fluchloralin, pendimethalum MCPA, Glyphosate, Propanil
- Non Selective herbicide – Kill all vegetation that they come in confact. Eg. Paraquat, Diquat.
- Systemic herbicide: Systemic herbicide move within the plant

Eg: Atrayine, simayibne, propanil, 2.4-D MCPA, Glypthocte Butachlor, Fluchloralin. etc.

- Contact herbicide – Kills plants when they come in contact with plants Eg. Diquat, Paraquat.
- Pre-emergence application – application of herbicide before the emergence of weeds. (c4) Paraquat, Diguat, 2.4-D, Propanil, Isoproturon, Glyphosate .
- Pre Planting incorporation – application of herbicide before sowing of crops eg. Fluchloralin.
- Soil sterilenths – (eg.) Diuron, Atrazine, Methyl bromide Effective herbicides on Monocotylidous weeds –

eg. Delapon, Fluchloalin.

- Herbicides which have low residual toxicity- Diquat paraquat
- Herbicides which have high residual toxicity – Diuron, Atrazine.
- Parasitic weeds - Weds which derives foods directly from the host plant
- Total stem parasite - Cuscuta associated with lucorn crop
- Partial stem parasite - Loranthus associated with tree crops
- Total root parasite - Orabanche associated with Tobacco
- Partial root parasite - Striga associated with sorghum
- Aquative weeds - Weeds growing in water bodies eg. Water hyacinth, hydrilla, Salvania, cattail weeds.
- **Allelopathy** – One plant having detrimental effect on other plants by releasing root chemical through roots.

CROPPING SYSTEM

- Mono Cropping – Growing of only one crop on a piece of land year after year
- Multive cropping – Growing two or more crops on the same piece of land in one calender year.
- Inter cropping – Growing 2 or more crops simultaneously with definite row arrangement.
- Sequential cropping- Growing at low or more crops in sequate on the same piece of land in a farming year.
- Zaid cropping – Growing of crops in between Kharif and rabbi season
- Jham/ shifting cultivation – The slash and burn type of cultivation in the hill treats of North Eastern Region.
- Catch crop – Quick growing crop incidentally planted and harvested in between two major crops, mainly to utilize residual fertilizer
- Cover crop – Crops which are grown primarily to cover the soil and to reduce the loss of moisture and eroion

- Multy storey cropping- system of growing together crops of different heights at the same time on the same piece of land (eg.) coconut + Pepper + cocoa + Pineapple

WEED MANAGEMENT

- Weed : is an unwanted plants, a plant out of place
- Classification of weeds

Based on duration:

a. Annuals – Complete their life eyclein one year eg. Phaloris monr, Echinocloa colonum, Amaranthus (Pig weed family)
b. Binneal weeds – complete their life cycle in five years (eg.) Alternanithra echinata; Eichorrutim intybus
c. © Perennial weeds – More than 2 years (eg.) cynodam dactylon, cyperus rotundus

CHAPTER EIGHT

PATHOLOGY

- Father of Plant pathology- **Anton De Bary**
- Father of Indian Plant Pathology- **E. J. Butler**
- An Indian whose name is associated with wheat rust- **K. C. Mehta**
- Irish Famine(1845)- Due to late blight of potato (*Phytophthora infestans*)
- Bengal Famine(1943)- Due to brown spot of rice (*Helminthosporium oryzae*)
- Father of plant virology- **Beijerinck**
- Father of plant Bacteriology- **E. f. smith**
- Most imp disease of rice- Blast *(Pyricularia oryzae)* controlled by Hinosan, Kitazin, Blasticidin, Beam.
- Kresek phase- Bacterial leaf blight of rice *(Xanthomonas oryzae)*
- Bakanae disease of rice (Foot rot)- *Gibberella fujikuroi* (Also known as Foolish seedling disease-symptom: plant become very tall)
- Sheath rot of rice- *Sclerotium oryzae*
- Rice Tungro- A virus transmitted by *Nephottetix virescens*
- Ufra disease of rice- By nematode *(Ditylenchus angustus)*
- Most pathogenic bacteria are gram negative and rod shaped
- Gram positive plant pathogenic bacteria: **Corynebacterium/ Clavibacter** (tundu disease of wheat)

- Tundu disease caused by- **Bacteria and nematode (*Anguina tritici)* association, a complex disease
- Plant viruses are mostly **single stranded RNA**
- Virus contain only one type of nucleic acid, either DNA or RNA, never both
- Virus contain nucleic acid 5 % and protein (nucleoprotein)- **95 % (TMV)**
- Tobacco mosaic virus is single stranded RNA- Rod shaped transmitted by sap or mechanically
- Single stranded DNA plant virus- **Gemini virus**
- Double stranded RNA virus- **Reovirus**
- Double stranded DNA virus- **Caulimovirus**
- Total stem parasite- **Cascuta (Dodder)**
- Partial stem parasite- **Loranthus**
- Total root parasite- **Orobanche**
- Partial root parasite- **Striga**
- Bacterial cell wall is made up of – **Murein/peptidiglycan**
- Karnal bunt of wheat discovered by- **Mitra et al., in 1931**
- A disease affecting wheat export from India- **Karnal Bunt (*Neovossia indica / Tilletia indica)***
- Wheat: a. Stem Rust (Black) - *Puccinia graminis tritici*- Alternate host: **Berberi (*Berberis vulgaris)*** b. Leaf rust (Brown) - *P. recondita*, Alternate host: **Thalictrum sp. c)** Stripe rust (Yellow)- *P. striiformis*
- Rust disease is controlled by **Plantvax**- a systemic fungicide
- Smut disease is controlled by- **Vitavax** (a systemic fungicide)
- Wheat rust in India survive in the southern hill (Nilgiri) and in Northern hill (Himalaya) in the form of Uredospore
- Loose smut of wheat- *Ustilago nuda tritici* (Internally seed borne, controlled by Vitavax, solar Heat Treatment)
- Molya disease of wheat- Nematode- *Heterodora avanae*
- Black arm of cotton- *Xanthomonas campestris pv. malvacearum*

- Red rot of sugarcane- *Collectrichum fulcatum*

- Grassy shoot- **Phytoplasma**
- Sporadic- Occurs irregularly in a place at low level
- Endemic- Occurs every year in a confined area at some level
- Pandemic- Occurs over a few countries or few continents
- Epidemic- Occurs over a large geographic area in short time at a devastative level
- Viroid- a plant pathogen made up of only RNA (single stranded). No protein is there
- Prions- Infectious protein molecule
- Potato- 1. Spindle tuber disease (1st discovered Viroid disease)
- Other Viroid disease- Coconut cadang cadang, Citrus exocartis
- Disease caused by Phytoplasma(MLO)- a. sandal spike b. sugarcane grassy shoot c. Brinjal little leaf d. Sesamum Phyllody e. coconut root wilt
- Disease caused by Spiro plasma (Phyllody)- **Citrus stubborn**
- Viral disease- Bunchy top of banana- *Pentalonia nigronervosa*
- Crown gall of stone fruit- *Agrobacterium tumefaciens*
- Fire blight- First bacterial disease discovered- *Erwinia amylovora*
- Ergot of Bajra- *Claviceps microcephala (purpurea)*
- Green ear disease of Bajra- *Sclerospora graminicola*
- Wart of potato and Golden nematode- Endemic pest, domestic quarantine
- *Bunt- Tilletia foetida. T. caries*
- Fungicide- Bordeaux mixture discovered by **Millerdat**
- Systemic fungicide- **Van Schmelling & Marshal Kulka**
- Pomegranate blight- *Xanthomonas campestris* pv. *punica.* Recently epidemic in Maharashtra
- Panama wilt of banana- fungal disease
- Moko disease of banana- Bacterial disease
- Soft rot of potato- *Erwinia carotovora*
- Kalisena- Bio formulation of *Aspergillus niger* N27 to control soil borne disease, developed in IARI

- Gene deployment for control of Rust- by **Nagarajan**
- Seed gall wheat- Nematode, Molya disease, *Anguina tritici*
- Destructive insect pest act- **1914**
- Cyanobacteria-BGA-prokaryotic
- Powdery mildew- controlled by **sulphur fungicide**
- Apple scab caused by- *Venturia inequalis* **(perfect)** *Spilocaea pomi* **(fungi)**
- Scab of potato caused by- *Steptomyces scabies* **(Actinomycetes)**
- Electron Microscope discovered by – **Knoll and Ruska (1932)**
- Crystallization of Virus – **Stanley (1935)**
- First book on plant pathology written by – **Julius Kuhn (1858)**
- Wart disease of Potato is endemic to **Darjeeling only**
- Plasmid – extra chromosomal fragments found in bacterial cells
- Gene to gene Hypothesis proposed by – **Flor (1955) in linseed rust**

PLANT PATHOLOGY IN INDIA:

- **K. R Kirtikar** was the first Indian scientist who collected many Fungi and identified them
- **E. J Butler (1910)** did detailed studies of Fungi and diseases caused by them. He wrote a book **'Fungi and Diseases in Plants'**
- **E. J Butler** is called the ' **Father of Modern Plant Pathology'** in India
- **J. F Dastur (1886-1971)** was the first Indian plant pathologist to study in detail on fungi and plant diseases

- **B. B Mundkar** identified and classified the smut fungi found in India

- The **Indian Phytopathological society** is founded by **B. B Mundkar in 1948**
- **Dr Karam chand Mehta (K. C Mehta)** of Agra college discovered disease cycle of cereal rust in India
- **Prof. Jaichand Luthra** and **Sattar** developed solar heat treatment technique of seeds to control loose smut in wheat
- **M. J Thirumalachar** performed extensive studies on rusts and smuts in India. Developed antibiotics like **Oreofungin** and **Streptocyclin**

Mycoplasma:

- Larger than viruses but smaller than Bacteria
- Devoid of cell wall and cytoplasm
- Enveloped by a lipo-protein plasma membrane
- Highly resistant against the antibiotic Penicillin but is sensitive to Tetracycline antibiotic
- Tetracycline used to control Mycoplasma
- First isolated from sheep infected by Pleuro pneumonia and therefore called PPLO (Pleuro pneumonia like organisms)
- Most of the yellow diseases of plants are caused by Mycoplasma
- E.g. Witches broom of Potato, Mulberry dwarf and Aester yellows etc.

Miscellaneous:

- **Virus** = Nucleic acid (DNA or RNA) + Protein (outer cover)
- **Lipo-virus** = Nucleic acid + protein + lipid **e.g. Influenza virus**
- **Animal virus (Bacteriophage)** = DNA + Protein
- **Plant virus** = RNA + protein
- **Viroid** = nucleic acid only
- **Plant Viroid** = RNA only

BACTERIOPHAGES:

- Discovered by F. W. Twort (1915) and Felix de Herelle (1917)
- Contains nucleic acid (double stranded DNA)
- It has two parts viz tail and head
- The tail is composed of protein only. The head has outer coat of protein and inner core as DNA

VIRIOD:

- Term 'viriod' used by T.O Diener
- Naked nucleic acids without protein coat
- Consists of only RNA

- These 'miniviruses' are the smallest known agents of infectious disease
- Potato spindle was the first disease reported to have been caused by a viriod
- Infectious in plants only
- Examples – Citrus excortis viriod, chrysanthemum stunt and chlorotic mottle viriod

Virions:

- Individual, completed and infectious nucleoprotein particles of a virus
- In short, virus particles are called Virions
- Also called nucleocapsids

Prions or slow viruses:

- Smallest proteinaceous infectious
- Contains protein only
- Example – Mad cow disease, Alzheimer's disease

- Nanometre is the unit for measurement of viruses

LIST OF RICE DISEASES

MAJOR FUNGAL DISEASES

Sr. No.	Disease	Causal Organism
1.	Blast	*Pyricularia grisea*
2.	Brown spot	*Bipolaris oryzae*
3.	False smut	*Ustilaginoidea virens*
4.	Kernel smut	*Tilletia barclayana*
5.	Leaf smut	*Entyloma oryzae*
6.	Sheath blight	*Rhizoctonia solani*
7.	Sheath rot	*Sarocladium oryzae*
8.	Stem rot	*Sclerotium oryzae*

MINOR FUNGAL DISEASES

Sr. No.	Disease	Causal Organism
9.	Sheath spot	*Rhizoctonia oryza*
10.	Stackburn (Alternaria leaf spot)	*Alternaria padwickii*
11.	Stem rot	*Sclerotium oryzae*
12.	Water-mold	*Fusarium spp., Pythium spp.*
13.	Black kernel	*Curvularia lunata*
14.	Pecky rice (kernel spotting)	*Cochliobolus miyabeanus, Sarocladium sp.*
15.	Root rots	*Fusarium sp., Pythium sp*
16.	Seedling blight	*Fusarium sp., Curvularia sp.*

CHAPTER NINE

GENETICS AND PLANT BREEDING

IMPORTANT POINTS:

- **1717**: Thomas Fairchild produced the first artificial hybrid popularly known as Fairchild's mule by crossing carnation with sweet William
- Dwarfing gene in rice – **Dee-Gee-Woo-Gen** (Japonica rice, Taiwan)
- Dwarfing gene in wheat – **Norin 10 (Japanese variety)**
- **Tift 23 A** – source of Cytoplasmic male sterility in pearl millet
- **Kafir 60** – source of CMS in sorghum
- Non-traditional area of wheat cultivation – **West Bengal**
- Non-traditional area of Rice cultivation – **Punjab**
- **Gregg 399** is an important source of genetic male sterility in cotton
- Exotic varieties of wheat – **Sonara 64 and Lerma Rojo**
- Wheat variety resistant to all the three rust – **sparrow**
- Wheat variety susceptible to all the three rust – **Agra Local**
- Exotic varieties of Rice – **Taichung Native 1 (TN1), IR 8** introduced in India in 1966
- Autotriploid (3x) – E.g. **banana**
- Triploid – **Apples, Watermelons, sugar beets**
- Autotetraploid – **potato**
- Autopolyploid – **ornamental plants, sweet potato, oat, alfalfa**

- Allopolyploids – **wheat, tobacco, cotton, sugarcane, rapeseed etc**
- Allohexaploid – **common bread wheat (*Triticum aestivum*)**
- Allotetraploids – **cotton and tobacco**
- Man made cereal – **Triticale (rye ×wheat)**
- **Maize** is called the **'Drosophila of crop plants'**
- Examples of secondary introduction – wheat: **kalyan Sona and Sonalika** selected from introductions from CIMMYT

Organelles	Structure	The chief function
* Cell wall	* Found between middle lamella and plasmalemmas * Have primary cell wall, secondary cell wall (3 layers) * Made up of cellulose microfibrills	Shape: strength and Rigidity
* Plasmamembrane	* Lipid – bilayer model of Davson Danieli, (1935) where protein molecule arranged outside	To regulate the movement of various molecules into & out of cytoplasm
* Neucleus (1993, Robert Brown) Nuclear membrane	* Double membrane with pores	* contains genetic material * Communteat with Cyptoplasm (ER)
* Chromatin * Nueleolus * Nucleoplasm	*Thread like (DNA + Nucleoprotein) * Globular synthesis	*DNA-genetic material * Site of RNA * With material for building DNA + MRNA
Cytoplasm * Ribosome	- 80s size (Animal & Plant) - 70s size (eukaryotic organelles) & prosktuyotes	Site of protein Synthesis
* Endoplasmic reticulum (ER) (Porter, 1948)	-Network like in cytoplasm rough (ER) with Ribosome Smooth (ER)-without Ribosome	* Protein Syn; aid in protein modification * Lipid synthesis site
* Mitochondria (Benda.) (Power house of cell)	* Cylindrical body dia: 0.2-1p length 3-10p * Inner folded membrane (Cristae) * Matrix inside	* Production of ATP through the kreb's cycle & electron transport chain * β-exudation of long chain fatty acids
* Plastid when Differentiated Chloroplast (With	* Biconvex lens shaped (5m*dia) * Have membranes (grana and stroma lamellae)	* Chlorophyll photosynthesis * Grara & storma lamellae

(Colourless plastid leucoplast)		* Storma consists of enzymes of dark reaction
* Golgi body apparatus/ dictyosome in plants (Camillo golgi. 1822)	* Membranes	* Shipment in transport vesicles (Packaging) & transport
*Lysosome (Duve. 1955) *Vacuole	* Sac of digestive enzyme / Digestive vacuoles * Membrane (Tonoplast) bound	* Cell destruction if captured * Storage deposit for water metabolites and product * turgidity of cell
* Centriole	Rarely present in Plants	Form poles of spindle apparatus
* Cytosol/ hyaloplasm	The fluid protein of cytoplasm exclusive of organelles	Have compounds for building macro molecules

STRUCTURE AND FUNCTION OF CELL ORGANELLES

- Ploidy Level in Seeds
- Embryo-2n Endosperm – 3n Testa-2n Aleuron –2n
- Post-mendalian era:
- devries, correns, Tschemark- Rediscovery of mendehan principles (1900).
- Sutton & bovery – chromosomal theory of inheritance (1903).
- Bateson –term – GENETICS (1905)
- Histones are – velly charged proteins on which –velly charged DNAs are coiled. 5 types of Histones are available.
- Hetro chromatin – Darkly stained Euchromatin – lightly stained
- -genetically inactive -genetically active
- Chromosome – named by waldayer –a neucleoprotein
- Chromosome – discovered by strasburger (1875)

- Parts of chromosome – (1) Centronere (2) Telomere (3) Nucleolar organising region
- Arms.
- Sources of new variation : (1) Independent assortment (2) Mutation (3) Recombination cause of C. over (d) Poly Ploidy (5) Somoclonal variation
- - Epitasis interallelic intraction (1909)
- Muller first used X-rays as mutagen
- Natural mutation is of low frequency 10^{-6}
- Muton – The unit in which mutation occurs
- Inbred- Progeny of a single cross fertilized heterozygous individual
- Xenia – effect of pollen on endosperm expression Metaxenia – effect of pollen on seed coat colour
- Pure lime are homozygous and hemogenons in nature
- Clone group of individuals descending from a single plant through several reproduction.
- X = Basic chromosome number = Monoploid number = Genome number n = Haploid number = Gametic number
- Genome – All the chromosomes of a diploid species that are distinct from each other with reference to gene content and morphology.
- Superiority of F_1 hybrids over both of its parents : *Heterosis*
- Isogenic lines: Two lines differing for a single locus
- Parthenogenesis: Embryo originates from unfertilized egg. Parthenocarpy : Development of fruit without fertilization , ex.: Banana
- Aneuloidy : Changes in the genome with reference to individual chromosomes. Ex. Monosome (2n-1), Trisomy (2n=1), Tetrasomy (2n=2)
- Euploidy : Changes in the genome with reference to a set of chromosomes genome. Ex.: Triploid-3x, Tetraploid- 4x.
- Test cross: F_1 x homozygous recessive parent.
- Backcross : Repeated crossing of hybrid progeny back to one of its parents

- Pleiotrophy : Single gene – governing multiple traits.
- Apomixis: A type of asexual reproduction in which embryo development and seed formation take place without fertilization and with or without meiosis.
- ex.: Triteum aestinum, 2n = 6x = 42 n = 21 (42/2), X = 7 (42/6)

CHAPTER TEN

SOIL SCIENCE

ROCKS:

- Earth crust consists of the elements Oxygen, silicon, aluminum, iron etc. in the decreasing order of their amounts.
- Rocks are basically divided into 3 types.
- **Igneous Rocks:** *Granite, Basalt (Deccan Trap), Gabbro, Pumice, Rhyolite and Tracheolite* Acidic igneous rocks contain 60-75% quartz *e.g.* granite. Basic igneous rocks contain less than 50% of quartz *e.g.* Basalt.
- **Sedimentary rocks:** *Limestone, sandstone, Shale, Dolomite and Conglomerate.*
- **Metamorphic rocks:** are formed from Igneous and sedimentary rocks *e.g. marble, gneiss, Schist, graphite, slate.*
- **Important conversions:** Gneiss is formed from Granite. Marble from Limestone, Graphite from Coal, Slate from Shale Quartzite from quartz or sandstone.

SOIL:

- **Soil Origin, Weathering, Morphology, Factors and Processes of soil formation**
- Rocks are the chief sources of soil parent materials over which soils are formed.
- Soil is formed from weathering of rocks.

Weathering = Disintegration + Decomposition

- Disintegration breaks consolidated rocks into unconsolidated parent materials, which on further breaking and chemical decomposition forms soil.
- Physical weathering involves agents such as temperature, *Water, wind, Plant and animals and* processes such as *exfoliation (surface peeling off of rocks), alternate wetting and drying, freezing and thawing, burrowing of animals, root penetration, etc.*
- Water, on freezing, expands 9% by volume.
- Chemical weathering reactions- Solution, hydration, Hydrolysis, carbonation, Oxidation and reduction.
- Hydrolysis is the most important chemical weathering process.
- Geo-chemical weathering is the weathering taking place at the layers down below whereas pedo-chemical or pedogenic weathering is the one taking place at the surface and subsurface layers.
- Soil found at the site of formation- sedentary soils, whereas soils found far away from the site of formation are called Cumulous or transported soils
- Agent of transportation & name of the soil formed: River water- Alluvium, Lake water- Lacustrine, Seawater-Marine, Wind-Aeolian if coarse and Loess if fine particles, Gravity-Colluvium, Ice-Moraine.
- Stages of soil formation- Infancy, youth, maturity and old age:
- Soil wherein there is continuous deposition of materials always remains young *e.g.* Desert soils and alluvial deposits.
- *Pedology* is the study of origin, formation and geographic distribution of soils in nature whereas *Edaphology* is the study of soil in relation to crop growth.
- *Soil profile* is the vertical section of soil through all its horizons and it extends up to its parent materials.
- A pedon is the smallest volume that can be recognised as a soil individual and it is e- dimensional.
- The horizontal layers in a soil profile are called horizons.

- Typically there are 4 horizons –O, A, B and C. O horizon is the organic horizon found in the forest soils. A horizon is below O horizon out of which A_2 layer is called illuvial horizon. B-horizon is found below A horizon and is mostly called illuvial horizon. Elluvial layer is the one wherein soil materials are removed whereas illuvial layer is one wherein soil materials removed from other layers are deposited.
- C- Horizon consists of unconsolidated parent materials.
- Below the C-horizon is found the R layer, which is known as the Bed Rock.

Solum = A+B horizons *Regolith* = A+B+C horizons

- The study of the soil in the field condition with the help of various morphological characteristics is called Soil Morphology.
- *Dokuchaiev,* the father of Soil science, gave the factors of soil formation, which were later, modified by *Jenny.*
- The five factors of soil formation are *Clorpi* – Climate and organism (Active factors), Relief or topography, parent material and time (passive factors).
- There are various processes of soil formation out of which two are important- Laterisation and Podzolisation.
- Laterisation occurs in warm humid tropical conditions whereas Podzolisation occurs in the cold humid temperate conditions.
- In Laterisation, Silica (SiO_2) is removed from the A horizon and sesquioxides are left out in the A-horizon whereas in Podzolisation, sesquioxides are leached from the A horizon and silica is left out in upper layers.
- Laterite is used for preparing bricks Laterites are very well weathered soils whereas laterite soils are still undergoing some weathering to become laterites.
- Nature and composition if soil:
- Soil is a *3-phase, particulate, disperse, porous, open and heterogeneous system*

- Ideal soil contains 50% solid matter (45% mineral matter and 5% organic matter) and 50% pore space (25% air and 25% water).
- Out of the 3 phases, Solid phase is the constant phase in terms of composition.
- There are basically 3 soil separates *viz.,* sand, silt and clay. There are two systems of classifying the sizes of these separates.
- International System given by *Atterberg* – Coarse sand 2mm – 0.2 mm, Fine sand 0.2mm to 0.02, silt – 0.02mm to 0.002mm and clay – less than 0.002mm or less than 2 microns.
- USDA system – Gravel – 2mm and more, Very coarse sand 2-1mm – 0.2mm, coarse sand – 1.0 to o.5mm, medium sand – 0.5 to 0.25mm, fine sand 0.25 to 0.1mm, very fine sand 0.1 to 0.05mm, silt 0.05 50 0.002mm and clay – less that 0.002mm.
- India follows International system of particle size classification.
- Physical properties of soil:
- The relative proportion of the various soil separates is called soil texture. There are 12 textural groups.
- Light textured or coarse textured soils are easy to plough whereas heavy textured or fine textured soils are difficult to plough.
- The 12 textural groups from light or coarse textured to heavy or fine textured soils is sand, loamy sand, sandy loam, loam, silt loam, silt, sandy clay loam, clay loam, silty clay loam, sandy clay, silty clay and clay.
- Gravel is neither a soil separate nor one of the soil textures.
- Particles greated than 2mm are not considered soil.
- Textured is determined by International Pipette and Bouycous Hydrometer method.
- Stoke's law is applied in the determination of soil texture.
- Silt has intermediate characteristics between sand and clay.
- Clay is called the active fraction of the soil. It is made up of alumino-silicates.
- Soil texture is a static property *i.e.* it cannot be changed.
- Soil structure is the arrangement of soil aggregates or primary and secondary particles.

- Grade denotes the durability or stability of the aggregates – structureless, weak, moderate, strong and very strong.
  Class of soil structure denotes size of the aggregates: very fine, fine, medium, coarse and very coarse.
- There are *4types* soil structures: platy, prismatic or columnar, angular or sub-angular blocky and spheroidal (granular and crumb structure).
- Structure is denoted in the order of GRADE-CLASS-TYPE.
- Structure of the soil can be easily changed by management practices.
- Loamy texture and granular or crumb structure is best suited for agriculture crops.
- Bulk density (Apparent density of soil is the mass of unit volume of soul including the pore space.
- Particle density (True Density) is the mass of unit volume of soil without pore space.
- Bulk density (A) is approximately half that of particle density. So bulk density is always lower than particle density value of Bulk Density is 1.4 to 1.8 Mg/m^3. Bulk density increases on compaction whereas it decreases on addition of organic matter.
- The particle density (T) of soils is around 2.65 Mg/m^3 due to dominance of quartz whose density is also of the same value.
- Porosity percentage pore space is given by the formula 100x(T-A/T).
- Values: Sandy soil +30% clay soils =50-60% and loams = 40-50%
- Macropores are greater in coarse textured soil and are occupied by air while micropores are greater in fine textured soils and are occupied by water.
- Soil colour:
- It is found out using Munsell Colour chart. Three variables are used to denote soil colour .They are hue-dominant Wavelength, Value-relative lightness of the colour and chroma-purity of the colour.
- Plasticity and cohesion:

- Plasticity is the capacity of the soil to change its shape under moist conditions.
- Cohesion is the capacity to stick together.
- Plastic soils are cohesive.
- Soil Colloids:
- The two phases are the dispersed phase (clay and humus) and dispersion medium/water).
- Soil colloid is made up inorganic colloid-clay and organic colloid-humus.
- Particles smaller than I micron are said to exhibit colloidal activity.
- Colloidal property increases with decrease in diameter.
- Colloids exhibit the property of sacrificial activity such as the capacity to hold solid, gases, salts and ions.
- Soil colloids have high exchange capacity, which increases with silica sesquioxides ratio.
- Soil water:
- Water has maximum density at 4^0 C. One molecule of water is attached to four molecules in the neighborhood. The diameter of water molecule is 3^0A ($3x10^{-10}$m). Water has high dielectric constant of 80. Its surface tension is $7.2x10^{-2}$N/m.
- Structure of water molecule is hexagonal lattice and the angle is 104^0 5^0.
- Soil moisture constants: Hygroscopic water, capillary water and gravitational water.
- Water held at tension of more than 31-atm is called hygroscopic water. It is not available to the plants.
- Water held below $1/3^{rd}$ –atm is called gravitational water and it is drained from the soil due to gravity.
- Water held at tensions beyond 15- atm is not available to the plants. 15 atm represents the wilting point.
  If water is allowed to drain by gravity after supplying water, some water remains even after drainage due to gravity. It is called field capacity. Water at field capacity is held at 1/3red atm.

- Water held between $1/3^{rd}$ and 15 atm is called available water
- Water in soil moves in response to difference to tension or pressure.
- More water means less tension and less water is held at more tension. So water moves from low tension to high tension.
- Darcy's law in soil deals to hydraulic gradient.
- Soil air:
- Soil air contains 10 times carbon dioxide as that of air.
- Ideally $2/3^{rd}$ of soil pores are filled with water and $1/3^{rd}$ with air.
- Fick's law deals about the diffusion of gases in soils.
- Submerged soils contain less oxygen.
- Soil air is characterised by ODR-Oxygen Diffusion Rate.
- Soil temperature:
- In soils, heat is mainly transferred through conduction
- Fourier's law deals with heat conduction in soils.
- *Sandy soils absorb more heat than clayey soils because the specific heat of water (heat required to heat a substance) is 4-5 times that of soil particles.*
- Soil temperature is used at family level categorization in soil taxonomy.
- Chemical properties:
- pH is the negative logarithm of H ion concentration. Sorenson gave pH scale.
- There are two types of acidity in soil-active acidity and potential acidity.
- pH measure only active acidity. Potential acidity forms the bulk of the soil acidity. It is greater than active acidity.
- Soil pH is also soil reaction.
- Soil with pH less than 6.5 are acidic, 6.5 to 7.5 are neutral and above 7.5 are alkaline.
- *One unit change in pH changes H ion concentration by 10 times, 2 units by 100 times and so on.*
- Electrical conductivity:
- Measure of soluble salts in mmhos/cm or dS/m in solubridge or conductometer.

- Ion exchange:
- Most important process occurring in soil Ion exchange is a reversible pros\cess. Soil colloids are the seat of ion exchange.
- Cation and anion exchange respectively. CEC is measured at pH 7 & expressed as meq/100 g of soil. CEC varies greatly with nature and amount of clay and OM.
- Knolinite has 3-10, Illite – 10-30, Montmorillionite – 80-150 and Organic matter – greater than 200.

$BS =\{(Na^+ +K^+ +Ca^{++} +Mg^+ +)/CEC\}x100$

Base saturation:

- Fertile soils are saturated with Ca^{++} and Mg^{++} ions. If soil is saturated with more than 15% exchangeable sodium, than that soil is called Alkali soil. If soil is saturated with H^+ ions. Then the soil is said to be base unsaturated or acidic.
- Organic matter:
- OM on decomposition by humification process gives humus. Humus is amorphous an nature. In India OM is very less because of tropical and sub-tropical climate.
- In hilly and altitudes, OM is above 1% in mangroves it is 10-30%.
- CN ratio of OM is 10:1 whereas that of Indian soils is 5:1 to 25:1 with an average of 14:1
- Histosols are called Organic soils.

- Organic matter decomposition stages: First sugars & starches followed by proteins followed hemicelluloses, cellulose and fatty acids and <u>finally lignin</u> and waxes.
- Biological properties:

Bacteria > Actinomycetes> Fungi > Algae

- The smell of soils after fresh showers is due to Actinomycetes.

- Bacteria occur in neutral to alkahne pH. Fungi in acid pH and Algae in shade areas.
- Symbiotic N fixer – Rhizobium in Legumes, Non-symbiotic or Free living is Arotobacter.
- In paddy algae or Azolla fixes N.
- The amount of N fixed is 50-150 Kg.
- In plant N is fixed as R-NH2, which is converted to ammonia. The ammonia is converted so nitrite first by Nitrosomonas or Nitrosococcus, followed by Nitrite to nitrate by Nitrobacter. This process is called Nitrification.
- Some of the nitrification Inhibitors are N-Serve and AM.
- Optimum condition for nitrification process is field capacity and pH above 5.
- Mineralogical Properties:
- There are primary, secondary, accessory and amorphous minerals.
- Primary mineral: Order of occurrenc

Feldspars> Quartz> Mica> Limestone> Hornblende and augite> Olivine and serpentine

- Serpentine is hydrated silicate of Mg.
- Secondary minerals:
- 1:1- one silica and one alumina layer. Kaolinite, Halloysite and Dickite
- 2:1 – Two silica and one alumina layer: Montmorillionite (expanding), Vermiculite (Slightly expanding) and Illite (Non-expanding and 15% of silica is replaced by Al^{3-} and K^+ ions) Illite is also called as hydrous mica.
- 2:1:1 or 2:2 – Chlorite. The crystal unit is composed of one 2:1 unit (like mica and Montmorillionite) and one octahedral unit, Brucite $\{(Mg_3 (OH)6\}$.
- Accessory minerals: B- Tourmaline, F-Topaz, P-Apatite, Ti-Rutile and Anatase.

- Amorphous clay mineral: Allophane. Found in Soil order Andosols.
- Negative charge is due to exposed surface of clay and isomorphous substitution.
- Soil survey, classification and soils of India:
- There are two types of soil survey- Reconnaissance soil survey and detailed soil survey.
- In RSS_1 1^9 = 1 mile. Toposheets of 1:50,000 to 1:1,00,000 or aerial photo of 1:25,000 or 1:50,000 is used. Observations are once at 3-6 Kms.
- DSS: 1^9 = 8 mile or 1^9 = 16 mile. Cadastral maps of 1:5000 to 1:8000 or Aeria: photo of 1:10,000 is used Observation are once at ¼ - ½ Km.
- Forest area is surveyed by RSS.
- Soil classification:
- India, from 1969, follows USDA's Comprehensive system of soil classification called soil Taxonomy. It is type of multi-category classification wherein there 6 categories: soil order, suborder, great group, sub-group, family and series.
- There 12 order and the lastly added 11th and 12th orders are Andosols and Gelisols respectively, Andosols are found in volcanic cruption areas and contains high content allophane. Gelisols are found in arctic regions.
- The two largest orders in India are Inceptisols followed by Entisols.
- Soil of India:
- Largest area is occupied by alluvial soils 75 Mha.

- Black soils 9Vertisols mostly), 72 Mha, are characterised by Gilgai (shining surface), Micro- relief (ups and down), self-churning, smectite (expanding clays) and they are the Russian equivalent of Chernozems.
- 2/3rd of TN is of red soil. the parent material for red soils is mostly granite.

- Laterite is older than lateritic soils. Laterites are the oldest or most weather soils.
- Laterite means brick.
- Desert soils come under Aridisols.
- Problem soils occupy 10 Mha. Saline soils- 7.2 Mha and alkali soils- 2.8 Mha.
- Problem soils are highest in UP.
- Saline soils are formed mainly in aird and semi-arid regions due to rising of salt level in the water table. Also it is due to secondary salinisation due to poor quality irrigation water.

Type of soil	pH	EC(dS/m)	ESP (%)
Saline	< 8.5	> 4	< 15
Alkali	> 8.5	< 4	> 15
Saline-Alkali	< 8.5	> 4	> 15

- Saline are called white alkali soils and are said to cause boron toxicity. Treated by leaching.
- Alkali soils are called black soils and are reclaimed by applying **Gypsum**
- Saline tolerant varieties: *rice, wheat, barley, maize, sorghum and millets.*
- Sensitive crops: *Pulses and oilseeds.*
- Acid sulphate soils: pH less than 3.5 due to Liydrogen Sulphide gas production, found in Kerala and Sunderbans. Causes AKiochi disease. Cat clays are associated with these soils.
- Acid soils have very low pH. Reclaimed by liming with limestone or calcite ($CaCO_3$), Dolomite $CaCO_3$. $MgCo_3$. $2H_2O$. slaked lime Ca (OH_2) and Burnt lime or quick lime CaO.

Soil Management:

- The optimum physical condition of the soil for crop growth is called soil tilth.
- Other practices are choice of crops, following land capability classification, conserve soil and water, avoid salinity, alkalinity and water-logging, adopt crop rotation especially with legumes, apply soil amendments and follow balanced fertilization.
- Soil Testing:
- Mainly to test the fertility status of the soil that is to find out the nutrient deficiencies and soil amendments.
- Half a Kg soil sample is taken and analysed for pH, total soluble salts by EC, Organic Carbon by Walkley and Black Method, Available N by alkaline permanganate method, avai P by Olsen's or Bray's Method, avai K by Neutral Normal Ammonium Acetate method.
- pH below 6 is termed acidic, 6-8.5 neutral to saline, 8.6 to 9 tending to be saline and pH above 9 is termed as alkaline.
- Total soluble salts: EC in dS/m: Below 1is normal, 1-2 critical for germination, 2-4 critical for growth of sensitive crops, above 4 injurious to most of the crops.
- Soil test report gives soil texture, pH, EC, OC, Avai NPK, Gypsum and Lime amount to be added, Green Manure/Compost in the Flooding and draining.

Nutrient	LOW	MEDIUM	HIGH
Organic carbon	Below 0.5%	0.5 – 0.75%	>7.5
Available N (Kg/ha)	<280	280-560	>560
Available P (Kg/ha)	10	10-25	>25
Available K (Kg/ha)	<110	110-280	>280

STATUS OF AVAILABLE NPK IN SOILS

Soil Fertility, manures and fertilizers:

- Soil productivity and fertility are synonymous terms. Soil productivity is soil fertility+ something.
- There are 16 essential elements for plant growth. There are divided into Macro and micronutrients based on the amount of plant uptake.
- Major nutrients consist of Primary elements. Beneficial elements are I, Se, Ga, AI.
- Ballast elements are AI and SI.
- Arnon gave the criteria for essentiality of the nutrients and Nicholas gave the term functional or metabolic nutrients.
- Law of minimum was given by Father of AG. Chemistry Leibig and Law of Diminishing Returns was given by Mitscherlich.
- Nutrient such as nitrate, chloride and sulphate are not absorbed by the soil colloids and remain mainly in the soil solution.
- Diffusion mechanism enables nutrient movement *without* the movement of water.
- It is the mechanisms predominant are supplying most of the P and K to plant roots.
- Nitrogen role: greenish colour, efficient utilization of P and K. Its def symptoms (yellowing) occur in the older leaves because of its high mobility, Def hastens maturity whereas toxicity delays maturity because of prolonged vegetative flush, succulent, leathery growth and also causes lodging. Toxicity also impairs the quality of barley, tobacco, sugarcane and fruits.
- Nitrogen is available both in anionic and cationic form.
- Phosphorus promotes root growth, new cell formation, formation of grains and maturation of crops, influences the vigour of plants and improves the quality of the crops, increases resistances to diseases, N fixing in legume crops. Its deficiency causes reddish or purplish discolouration of stem and foliage due to abnormal increase in the sugar content and formation of anthocyanin.
- Potassium: to resist pest and diseases, cold and adverse conditions, starch production and production and translocation of sugars, improves the quality of tobacco and citrus. *Luxury*

consumption is noticed. Deficiency symptoms ringing of alfalfa leaves with rows of small white spots: reddish brown discolouration of cotton leaves, drying, scorching and curling of leaf margins in potato and 'interveinal chlorosis and 'firing' along the edges of maize leaves.

Nitrogenous fertilizers:

- Sodium Nitrate: 1st nitrogenous fertilizer. Chilean Nitrate 16% N in nitrate form. Particularly useful in acid soils
- Ammonium sulphate: 20.6% and 24% S. When close to seeds affects seed germination
- Anhydrous Ammonia contains highest N content of 32%.
- Urea contains 46% N and non-proteined organic form of N, amide form of N_1.
- Ammonium nitrate: 33-35% N (half as nitrate form and other half as Ammonical form), acidulating and explosive.
- Nitro-chalk is obtained by mixing Ammonium nitrate with about 40% limestone or dolomite. It has 20.5% (50% in Ammonical form and 50% in Nitrate form).
- Ammonium Sulphate Nitrate: Ammonium Nitrate + Ammonium sulphate. Contains 26% N (3/4th in Ammonical form and 1/4th in nitrate form.
- Ammonium chloride: 26% N, possesses good physical condition, similar in action to ammonium sulphate, not recommended for tomatoes, tobacco and other such crops.
- CAN: Calcium Ammonium Nitrate Kisankad 25-28% N (1/2 ammonical and ½ nitrate).
- Slow release N fertilizers: Neem coated urea, Tar coated urea, urea formaldehyde (urea form), Urea super granules, etc.
- Dried bone meal – 10-12% highly available N.
- Phosphatic fertilizers:
- Rock phosphate: 25-35% water Insoluble Phosphoric acid. Bone meal contains 20- 25% P_2O_5.

- Super Phosphate: Most widely used water-soluble P fertilizer in India. SSP: 16-18% P_2O_5, DSP-32% P_2O_5, TSP-44-49% P_2O_5.
- Citrate soluble P: Dicalcium phosphate- 35-38% P_2O_5 Basic slage –6-20% P_2O_5 byproduct of steel industries.
- Gypsum: 20% S and 23% Ca.
- Potassic Fertilizers:
- India imports K fertilizers mainly from Germany and France.
- MOP: KCI 50-63% K_2O
- SOP:K_2SO_4 48-52% K_2O.
- Wood ash – 5-6% Potassium carbonate.
- Complex fertilizer:
- Diammonium Phosphate: (DAP) – 18:46:0
- Suphala: Nitro phosphate – 20:20:2, 15:15:15, 18:18:9.

Manures:

- FYM has 0.3%, 0.15%, 0.3% N, P_2O_5 and K_2O.
- 1 tone of cattle dung can give only 2.95 Kg of N, 1,59 Kg of Phosphoric acid and 2.95 Kg of potash.
- Night soil is also called Poudrette.
- Soil erosion and conservation:
- Soil degradation is defined as the loss in soil productivity due to physical, chemical and biological deterioration.
- Causes are excessive pressure on land to meet the growing demands of population . They are in the form of over exploitation of natural resources like overgrazing, excessive deforestation, faulty methods of agricultural practices, shifting cultivation or Jhuming.
- There are 2 types of soil erosion Normal crosion (geological crosion) and Accelerated erosion.
- In normal erosion, rate of soil loss = rate at which soil is formed.
- Accelerated crosion is one where rate of soil of loss is far greater than the rate at which it is formed.
- Area affected by soil degradation is 187.9 Mha (57.1%) of the total geographical area.

- Deterioration in the form of water erosion (148.9 Mha), Wind erosion (13.5 Mha), chemical deterioration – 13.8 Mha, Physical deterioration like water logging (11.6 Mha) and Biological deterioration.
- Water erosion: Erosion by water – splash erosion, sheet, rill, gully, stream bank and landslide erosion.
- Splash erosion is the splashing effect of raindrops on soil particles.
- Sheet erosion is not clearly recognised but can be seen as muddy run-off.
- Rill erosion leads to formation of finger like rills and gully crosion is the severe form of rill erosion wherein grooves form deep channels called pullies. Land becomes unfit for cultivation.

- The mechanism of water crosion is *detaching effect* of raindrops and surface flow of water *carries* the detached soil particles to far places.
- Wind erosion:
- Wind erosion normally occurs in arid and semi-arid regions.
- 3 types of soil movement are seen in wind crosion : saltation, suspension and surface creep.
- Saltation is the most important process in wind erosion and control of wind erosion is mainly based on elimination of movement in saltation. Particles of size 0.1 to 0.5mm are lifted.
- Major portion of soil carried by wind is moved in a series of bounces called saltation.
- Suspension: Very fine particles less than 0.1mm in diameter are carried into suspension over long distances. They are kicked up into air by action of particles in saltation.
- Surface creep: Particles larger than 0.5mm but smaller than 1.0mm are pushed and spread along the surface by impact of particles in saltation to form a surface creep.
- The mechanism of wind erosion is Initiation, transportation and deposition.
- Factors affecting soil loss:

- Universal soil loss (USLE) was given Weischmeir and Smith.
- A= RKLSCP where A denotes soil loss in the , R-Rainfall erosivity, K-soil erodibility, L-slope length, S-slope%, C-crop management factor, P-Soil Management factor.
- Soil loss is calculated by comparing soil loss with an ideal plot of 22m long (72 ft) and 9% slope.
- Intensity of the rainfall is more important than duration and frequency of rainfall in causing soil loss.
- Soil texture, structure, infiltration, permeability, organic matter content etc affects soil erosion.
- *Lateritic soils are less erodible than black soils.*
- Speed and extent of run-off is decided by slope% and length.
- Velocity of water flow is proportion to square root of slope% or vertical drop.
- Hence if land slope% is increased 4 times then velocity is doubled.
- If velocity is doubled, erosive power of How is increased by 4 times *i.e.* erosive power is proportional to square of the velocity.
- Size of the particles carried by the flow is proportional to the 6th power of the velocity of flow. If velocity is doubled, size of the particles carried is increased by 64 times.
- Quantity of soil transported is proportional to the 5th power of the velocity of flow. If velocity is doubled, then quantity of soil transported is increased by 32 times.
- So erosion is geometrically increasing with slope%.
- Loss of plant nutrients increases with increase in degree of slope.
- Soil loss is less when land is left undisturbed under a natural cover and soil loss increases steeply when vegetation is removed and land is cultivated.
- Legumes and grasses are stronger in preventing soil loss.
- Monoculture of cereals should be avoided.

Soil And Water Conservation Measures

- The key to soil and water conservation is to follow land capability classification
- Land capability classes are based on intensity of hazards and limitations. As class increases, the intensity of limitations increases.
- Class V has no crosion hazard but it is placed in class V only due to the fact that it limitations are practically difficult to remove.
- Class VIII includes Bad Lands rock outcrops, sandy beaches, marshes, deserts, river washes, mine spoils and other nearly barren lands.
- The colours for the various classes from I to VIII are Green, yellow, Brown, Pink, Grey, Orange, Red and Purple.
- Sub class indicates dominant limitation and is denoted by e, w, s, c – e for erosion, w for wetness, s for soil limitations and c for climate.
- If two limitations are found, the dominant limitations are written first.
- The order of priority in case of equal extent of limitations is e, w, s, and c.
- Arid lands start with class IV, semi-arid with class III or IV, sub-humid where crop yield is affected frequently by drought with II or III, Humid climate with occasional dry spells with II and humid climate with well distributed rainfall with CLASS I.
- Soil and water conservation measure are divided into Agronomic and Engineering measures.

Agronomic measure:

The principles are to intercept raindrops and stop splash effect, to increase intake rate and to stop overland flow.

1. Contour farming: It is farming across the slopes along the contour bunds within 6% slope, Important examples of soil loss: Maize + cow pea (Contour cultivation) < maize (up and down cultivation).

Potato (contour cultivation) < Potato (up and down cultivation)

2. *Mulching:* synthetic and natural.

3. *Selection of crops:* crops selected should provide maximum cover of soil. Legumes are very effective particularly cowpea and mung. Crops can be divided into crosion resistant (Ground Nut) and crosion permitting crops (URAD).

Important *e.g.* of soil loss: Urad > Maize > Gora paddy > G. Nut.

Jowar > Black gram > G. Nut.

Biditobacco- fallow > Sun hemp- Biditobacco-fallow> Bajra-fallow> Bajra-Mung.

4. *Strip cropping:* Alternate strips of erosion resisting and erosion permitting crops.

Wind strip cropping is growing alternate rows of tall and short crops across the direction of wind.

5. *Mixea cropping:* Better protection and yield than strip cropping.

- **Engineering measures**: To increase the opportunity time and to divide the long slopes into short ones so that the velocity of flow is reduced.
- The methods are basin listing using basin leister (excavate some soil to allow rain water to enter), sub-soiling (to remove the surface hard pans),contour bunds upto 6% slope, graded bunds in rainfall areas with a vertical interval of 0.3 (s+3) where S is slope %, Bench terracing (series of benches or platforms, Grassed waterways using Pannicum repans, Brachaeria mutical or cyanodon.
- *Gully control measures:* Check dams, sodding, Gully plugging with brush woods, wire meshes, sand bags, boulders, live hedges (Vetiver), bricks masonry items, *etc* earthen plugging.
- In case of small gullies, diversion check bunds and in case of medium gullies, cheek dams at vertical interval of 1.2m and terracing the side slopes are done.

Soils of India

1. Red Soils (Alfisols):

- Red colour in red soils due to the presence of various oxides of iron
- Light texture, porous structure, deficient in organic matter
- Absence of lime and low soluble salts
- Slightly acidic to neutral in reaction
- pH ranging from 6.0 to 7.5
- Rich in Kaolinite (1:1) type of clay minerals
- Formed from ancient crystalline and metamorphic rocks
- The parent material for red soils is mostly granite
- It covers an area of 117.2 m ha (36 %)
- Distribution – Areas of Madras and Mysore, part of A.P, M.P, Orissa, Bihar, Santhal paragana (Bihar) , Mirzapur, Jhansi district of U.P
- Red soil in Tamil Nadu occupies the largest area.

2. Black soils (Vertisols) :

- Covers an area of about 74 m ha accounting for 24 % of the total geographical area
- Generally rainfed
- The soils are dark or dark brown in colour
- Developed from Basaltic rock under semi arid condition
- The soils are locally known as 'Regur' or black cotton soil, deep black soil, and medium black soil.
- The texture ranges from sandy loam to heavy clay.
- One of the characteristics of the swells on wetting during the season and shrinks and cracks in summer season
- The base exchange capacity of deep black soil is quite high
- The pH varies from 7.5 to 8.5
- The soils are deficient in nitrogen and phosphorus and they are rich in potash and lime
- The clay content ranges from 40-69 % and occasionally upto 80 %

- Cation exchange capacity is 35-50 meq/100g soil
- Rich in montmorillonite and beidelithoc group of clay minerals
- **Occurrence** – Maharashtra, Gujarat, M. P, Rajasthan, U.P, A.P and Madras

3. Alluvial soils (Entisols):

- Soils of recent origin
- It is grey or greyish- brown in colour and texture of alluvial soils is sandy loam to clay loam
- Most fertile soil
- Base exchange capacity is comparatively low and pH varies from 7.0 to 8.0
- Occupies the largest area i.e. 75 m ha

- The alluvial soils are found in the areas of Rajasthan, Punjab, U.P, Bihar and West Bengal
- Sufficient in P and K but deficient in Nitrogen and organic matter

4. Laterite and lateritic soils (Ultisols):

- Occupy 25 mha of the total geographic area
- Texture of top soil is loamy or clayey.
- Associated with undulating topography in region with a relatively high annual rainfall
- It is deficient in lime and are slightly to moderately acid in reaction
- The pH values from 5.0 to 6.0
- They are low in base exchange capacity
- Laterites are the oldest or most weather soils
- Predominate in Kaolinite type of clay minerals
- Deficient in P, K, Ca, Zn, B etc
- Shifting cultivation is mainly practised in these areas

5. Desert soils (Arid soils):

- Covers an area of about 29 m ha
- Developed in Arid regions. It is mostly sandy
- Desert soils contain large amount of soluble salts and varying proportion of lime
- They have a high pH and are very poor in fertility constituents
- Composed of Quartz but feldspar and horn blend grains also occur with a fair grains also occur with a fair proportion of calcareous grains
- Desert soils are largely found in parts of Rajasthan, South Punjab and in the range of Kutch.

6. Saline and Alkaline soils:

- Developed in the arid and semi arid regions
- Poor drainage is also responsible for their development
- Saline are called Alkali soils and are said to cause Boron toxicity. Treated by leaching
- Alkali soils are reclaimed by applying Gypsum
- Pulses and oilseeds are very sensitive to this soils
- Saline soils occupies 7.2 m ha and alkali soils – 2.8 m ha
- Highest in Uttar Pradesh
- pH is greater than 8.5
- Difficult to manage
- Exchangeable sodium percentage is more than 15
- Electrical conductivity is more than 4 mm hos/cm
- Occurrence- Indo-gangetic alluvium in the north and the deltic region

7. Forest and Hill soils:

- Estimated to be 75 m ha

- Occurrence –Himachal Pradesh, J& k, U. P, Uttarakhand, Bihar , Maharashtra, Kerala and North Eastern Region

Important points to remember:

- Soil profile – A vertical section of the soil body which shows different layers
- Soil texture – The relative proportion of sand, silt and clay
- Soil structure – Arrangement of soil particles e.g., granular, columner, compact
- Solum – A+B horizon
- Regolith – A+B+C horizon
- A well developed soil have : A, B, C horizon
- The most abundant soil found in India is alluvial soil
- Anion exchange capacity is found maximum in the case of – Kaolinite
- Cation exchange capacity is found minimum in the case of – Kaolinite
- Black soil is the second largest group of Indian soils
- Cation exchange capacity is highest in – Montmorillonite
- Denitrification is more in water logged soils
- In no tillage systems, the surface soil layers have high bulk density
- Lime is used for reclamation of acidic soils
- Maximum absorption of water by roots takes place through the root hairs
- Maximum population of microorganisms found in soils are – Bacteria
- Most resistant mineral present in soil is – Quartz
- Montmorillonite (2:1), illite and Kaolinite (1:1) are clay minerals
- Pedology – study of soil development
- Gypsum or sulphur is used for reclamation of saline soils
- The most abundant mineral present on the earth is Feldspar

- pH – the negative logarithm of hydrogen ion concentration in the soil
- Tolerance of soil salinity in crops – Barley> wheat > Beans>Upland paddy
- Igneous rock- Granite, Basalt; Sedimentary rocks – sandstone, Limestone, Dolomite; Metamorphic Rocks – marble, slate
- Check basin irrigation method is best suited for undulating topography
- Red soils are best suited for irrigated agriculture
- Carbon: Nitrogen (C:N) ration of normal soils -10-12:1
- The maximum moisture is available to plants at field capacity
- The main source of heat for soils is solar radiation
- Number of master horizons in soil are -5
- Micronutrient defiant in Indian soils – Zinc
- Fertilizers not produced in India – Muriate of Potash
- Degree of soil salinity is indicated by its Total soluble salt content
- Maximum saline and alkali soils are found in Uttar Pradesh
- Alkali soils are generally found in Arid and semi-arid climate
- **Gravitational water** is less available for plant or not available (-0.1 to –0.3 bar)
- **Capillary water**- water held between –0.1-31 bars, most available for plant growth, capillary water held between –15 bar is easily available to crop production
- **Hydroscopic water**- water is held below permanent wilting point, except few microbes, all plants fail to absorb hydroscopic water.
- Dark colour of soils is due to presence of Titanium and Mn
- Total essential nutrients – 17. Recently added mineral is 'Ni'.
- Ultra micro nutrient – Molybdenum
- Among the soil fauna, protozoa are the most abundant
- Edaphology – Study of relationship between plant and soil
- Petrology – study of Rocks

CHAPTER ELEVEN

AGRICULTURAL EXTENSION

- Ext. Education is the process of bringing desirable changes in human behaviour
- Grow more food campaign (1947)
- Grow more food enquiry committee (1952)
- Etawah pilot project, Etawah dist. of UP, (1948), fore runner of community dev. Project in India, started by Albert Mayer
- Community Dev, project (1952)
- National extension service (1952)
- Panchayat Raj System (PRS), Balwant Roy Mehta committee, introduced PRS (3 Tier, Dist->, Block->, Village), 2 Tier by Ashok Mehta committee.
- First Agricultural University as SAU, G.B.Pant AU. (1960), Uttaranchal
- IADP (Intensive Agr. Dev. programme)—1960
- IAAP (Intensive agri. Area Prog.)--- 1964
- HYVP (High yielding variety prog.) for wheat and paddy-1965-66
- SFDA (Small Farmer Dev. Agency)--- 1971-72
- Rural Credit Review Committee--- 1960
- NDP (National Demonstration project.)- 1960
- DAAP (1970-71) forth five year plan
- Drought prone area programme – 1970-71

- Command area development programme - 1974
- Tribal area development Programme- 1972
- Training and Village system--- 1974
- KVK—(first was in Pondicherry, TNAU) Teaching by doing, 1974
- TRYSEM (Training Rural youth for self employment)—15th Aug. 1979
- IRDP(integrated rural development program me) ---2nd Oct.1980-81
- JRY (Jawahar Rojgar Yojana) started by Merging National Rural employment prog and Rural Landless employment guarantee prog---------------- 1989
- Employment Assurance Scheme.—Oct 1993
- ICAR started IVLP (Institute village linkage prog.)—1995
- Forming System Research Extension- 1970
- Lab to land Programme and National Agricultural Research Project (NARP) – 1979
- National Agricultural Technology Project (NATP) – 1998
- National Agricultural Innovation Project (NAIP) – 2006
- Important Projects and Associated Persons

Name of Project	Associated persons
Gurgaon project	F.L Brain
Shantiniketan	Rabindranath Tagore
Rural Reconstruction	Daniel Hamilton
Marthandom Project	Spencer Hatch
Sewagram	Mahatma Gandhi
Etawah pilot project	Albert Mayor(first project)
Nilokheri experiment	S.K Dey
Majdoor Manjil	S.K Dey
Community Development	S.K Dey
Indian village scheme	S.N Gupta
National Demonstration scheme(NDS)	Kalwar and Subramaniam
Young farmer association	Deskmukh
3 tier Panchayat Raj(first in Rajasthan)	B.R Mehta
2 tier Panchayat Raj(first in Kamataka)	Ashok Mehta
T & V system	Daniel Benore

Important Projects and Associated Persons

CHAPTER TWELVE

AGRICULTURAL ENGINEERING

- Father of agricultural engineering in India – Professor Mason Vaugh
- First bachelor's degree course in agricultural engineering in India – Allhabad agricultural Institute ,Allahabad (1942-43)
- Indian society of agricultural engineers (ISAE) – 1960 at IIT Kahargpur and presently its headquarter is at New Delhi
- ISAE publications: 1) Journal Of Agaricultural Engineering (JAE)

Agricultural Engineering Today (ATE)

- 1960- 61 – atractor manuufacturing started in india by first manufacture m/s eicher good earth
- Average man can develop maxium power of about 0.1hp (74.6 watts) for doing farm work
- Power developed by an average pair bullocks is about 1hp (746 wants) for usual farm work
- The averge force a draft animal can exert is nearly one –tenth of its body weight
- Unit power availavle for crop production (india) is about 1.35 kw/ha but for desirable level of agricultural production power requirment could about 2.15 kw/ha

- Thermal efficiency for diesel engine – 32 to 38%
- Thermal efficiency for petrol engine – 25 to 32%
- Of the total energy produced in india the share of thermal power is about 56%,hydro electrical
- Power (36%) ,nuclear power(16%) and rest comes from deisel and gas based power.
- The farm holding in india are classified as (a) marginal(<1ha),(b) small(1-2 ha) , (c) semi medium (2-4ha) ,(d) medium (4-10),(e) large(>10 ha)
- At present agricultural machinery population is estimated at about 150 million which includes about 3 million tractor .(2.5 lakh tractor/year ,10000 power tiller /year)
- The most popular tractor is found in 31-40 hp segment , which accounts for 60% of the total sales in the country

Biogas

- Biomass: mixture of methane (45-70%) and carbon dioxide(30-35%)
- Cattle dung : water ratio for biogas slurry : 4:5or 1:1
- Buffaloes : 15 kg dunr/day, bullocks or cows : 10 kg dung /day and calves : 5kg dung/day
- Suitable condition for biogas production – ph(7-8), temperature(35 c)
- Biogas calorific value -4500 kcal/m^3

Wind energy

- The speed required for operation of wind mill – 10 to 15 km/hr
- Two types of wind mill (horizontal axis and vertical axis rotr)

1. Horizontal axis rotor –axis of rotion is parallel to the direction of wind i . Multi blade

   i. Propeller – most commonaly used

   ii. Sail type

2. Vertical axis rotor axis of rotation is perpendicular to the direction of wind

   - Components of wind mill :- tower ,head ,roto ,transmission gear ,pump,generator
   - Power available wind mill depends upon (1) wind speed (2) cross section of wind swept by rotor

3. Overall conversion efficiency of rotor , transmission system,generator Solar energy

   - Temperature of sun 5777 k
   - Radition range from sun ,0.4 um – maximum available range,
   - <0.4 um – ultraviolet radiation (8% of radition), 0.4-0.7 um visible radiation (46%)
   - >0.7 um infrared radiation (46%)

   - Solar constant : solar radiation received per second by surface of unit area held normal to the direction of sun rays at mean earth –sun distance. Its value 1350 w/m^2 or 1.94 cal/s/m^2
   - Radiation measurement
   - Pyrheliometer : beam radiation (direct radiation)
   - Pyranometer : total radiation (global radiation)- accurate
   - Solarimeter : total radiation (global radiation)- inaccurate
   - Pyrometer: very high temp measurement
   - Collection of solar radiation (three ways)

2. By flat plate collector : temp range 40 centigrade to 100 centigrade
3. Focussing or concentrating colletore (>100 °c)
4. Photovoltaic cell (soller cell) : directly convert solar energy in to electricity made of Silicon separated by thin brrier with

conversion efficiency is about 10%

- Portable water contained <550 ppm of salt ,sea water contained 30000-40000 ppm of salt ,groundwater contained<2000-3000 ppm of salt
- Solar still –device converts saline water in to portable water.
- Green house is structure made of polythene/rain forced fibre to provide controlled condition for crop production

CHAPTER THIRTEEN

AGRICULTURAL PHYSICS

SUN AND THE EARTH SYSTEM

- The sun is a star and is a part of the Milky Way Galaxy. Sun rotates in an anti- clockwise direction *i. e.* from west to east. The temperature at the surface of the sun is around 6000C.
- The earth is at a mean distance of 150 million km from the sun. The mean surface temperature of the earth is 15 C.
- the shortest distance between the sun and the earth is called perihelion (147 million km) occurring on 3rd January and the longest distance is called Aphelion (152 million km) occurring on 4th July.
- *Solar constant* is defined as the total amount of solar radiation received per unit area per init time in the absence of atmosphere, the radiation being perpendicular and the earth at its mean distance from the sun. its value is 1.94 cal/cm2/min or 1.94 Langley/min.
- There are four seasons in a year namely winter solstice (2nd Dec), Spring equinox (21 March), summer solstice (Jun 21st) and autumn equinox (23rd September).
- During equinox, the sun is at the equator during solistices, the sun is at either tropic of cancer (summer solistice) or Capricorm (winter solistice).

ATMOSPHERE AND ITS COMPOSITION

- The vast expanse of air , which envelops the earth all around, is called the
- *atmosphere.*
- It can be broadly divided into four layers namely troposphere (upto 18 km in the equator and 8 km in the poles), stratosphere (8 or 18 km – 50 km), mesosphere (50km- 80km) and thermosphere (80km- 400km).
- Pure dry air constitutes mainly of nitrogen (78%), oxygen (21%), Argon (0.93%). Co_2 (0.03%), hydrogen, helium, water vapor, ozone, dust particles, smoke, salts and other impurities.
- Like a green house, it allows short wave radiation to enter into it and reach the earth's surface but is nearly opaque to long wave terrestrial radiation from the sun *(Green House Effect)*
- Some of the important Green house gases are CO_2 CFC^1s- Chlorofluorocarbons, CH$ Nitrous oxide, etc.,
- The atmosphere protects the earth from the harmful radiation of the sun with the help of the Ozone (O3) layer

METEOROLOGY AND CLIMATOLOGY (WEATHER AND CLIMATE)

- The study of envelope of air surrounding the planet and of the phenomena associated with the atmosphere is called <u>Meteorology</u>.
- A component of Meteorology is the study of weather. Weather is the present condition of the atmosphere at a particular. It is mainly concerned with its day-to- day effects on life and human activities.
- *Climatology* is the study of long-term manifestations of the weather represented by a statistical collection of weather conditions over a specific length of period usually at least a few decades.
- The use of science of Meteorology for agriculture is called *Agricultural Meteorology.*

- The various elements that combinedly express weather are air pressure and wind, temperature. Relative Humidity, precipitation (rainfall, snow, fog, hails, etc), visibility.
- The climate is controlled by four factors called *Climatic controls* – Astronomical factors, Geomorphological factors, solar factors and Anthropogenic factors.
- The Nine Climatic controls are latitude, altitude, distance from the sea, land and sea distribution, semi-permanent pressure system, storm tracks, occan currents, mountain barriers and air masses.

WEATHER ELEMENTS
Pressure:

- Atmospheric pressure is the weight of the column of air at any given place and time.
- It is measured by means of an instrument called (Aneroid) Barometer. It is measured as force per unit area. The units used by meteorologists for this purpose are called millibars (mb). One millibars force of one gram on a sq. cm. A pressure 1000mb = weight of 1.053 kg. Sq. cm. Normal pressure at sea level is 76 cm (1013.25 mb).
- An Isobar is an imaginary line joining places of equal atmospheric pressure reduced to sea level.
- On the earth's surface there are seven pressure belts. They are equatorial low (the doldrums) the sub-tropical high (horse latitudes) the sub-polar low and the polar high. Except the equatorial low, all others have matching pairs in the Northern and the Southern Hemisphere.

Wind:

- Horizontal movement of air is called wind. The vertical movement of air is called air current
- Lines joining places of equal wind speed are called Isotachs

- Winds of high speed are called Squalls.
- Due to horizontal differences in air pressure. air flows from areas of high pressure to areas of low pressure.
- Wing direction is determined with the help of a wind vane and the speed or velocity of the wind by Robinson's Cup Anemometer. In a wind vane. The head denotes the direction from which the air is blowing and the tail denotes the direction to which the air blowing.
- The two most well understood and significant winds for climate and human activities are the 'trade winds' and the 'westerly winds'.
- Winds which blow throughout the year from one latitude to other in response to the latitudinal differences in air pressure are called prevailing winds or planetary winds (*e.g.* Trade Winds)
- The winds blowing from sub-tropical high-pressure areas (30 N and S latitude) towards the equatorial low-pressure belts are the extremely steady winds known as the trade winds. They blow from west to east.
- Near the equator, the trade, winds clash with each other and on the line of convergence, they rise and cause heavy rainfall.
- The Westerlies are the winds blowing from the sub-tropical high-pressure belts towards the polar low-pressure belts. They blow from southwest to northeast in the Northern Hemisphere and from northwest to southeast in the southern Hemisphere.
- The westerlies are best developed between 40 and 60 latitudes. These latitudes are called 'roaring forties', 'furious fifties' and 'shrieking sixties'.

Periodic winds:

- The winds that reverse their direction periodically with season are called periodic winds. The monsoons are the best example of large-scale modifications of the planetary wind systems.
- The word monsoon is derived form the Arabic word 'Mausim' which means season.

- The monsoon winds thus refer to wind systems that have a pronounced reversal of direction.
- In India, 80-90% of the rainfall is obtained from two monsoons namely southwest Monsoon and "North East' or "Retreating monsoon'.
- Normally, the southwest monsoon reaches the Kerala Coast by the end of May, advances along the Konkan coast in early June and extends over the entire country by the end of July. The rains continue up to the end of September, when the southwest monsoon recedes.
- In November and December, Northeast monsoon is the main contributor of rain over the southeastern part of the peninsular region especially Tamil Nadu.
- The monsoon depressions can be said to be the single factor that controls the distribution of rainfall over the whole of India. These low-pressure systems. Which originate near the head Bay of Bengal and travel across the country in a west and northwesterly direction.
- Heavy rainfall mainly occurs to the south of the tracks of these depressions. 3 to 4 depressions are found in a month during these monsoons.
- When they take a normal Northwesterly track, there is flood in the Northern India and drought in the peninsula. When they follow an abnormal track across central India, there is flood in the Peninsular parts and drought in the Northern part of India.
- These depressions terminate in Gujarat and Rajasthan. When a depression reaches these states. They get abundant rains; otherwise they are subject to a prolonged drought.
- Occasionally there are one or two monsoon breaks during the monsoon seasons. These types of breaks normally bring floods in the rivers of Northern Bengal and Bihar.

Thunderstorms and Hails:

- Nimbostratus clouds indicate thunderstorms.

- Sudden change in the weather of particular place with heavy downpour is called thunderstorms and hail is rain in the form of ice crystals. Thunderstorms and hail are predominant weather phenomenon before and after monsoon seasons. Important ones are *Kalbaisakis* in Bengal and *Andhis* over North West India.

Cyclonic storms:

- Caused due to the creation of low-pressure zones. They cause severe damage to the coastal zoos on an average 2-3 storms may be expected in a year.
- They are associated with the high wind speeds and tidal winds

Western Disturbances

- Series of disturbances in the form of cloudy weather and light rainfall in the plains and snow fall in the hills.
- These disturbances affect the Rabi crops.

Rainfall:

- Line joining places of equal rainfall are called Isohyets.
- Most of the rainfall of India is obtained from the Southwest and North East Monsoon seasons.
- The constancy by which a place receives rainfall is studied with the help of *Co- efficient of variation (CV)*. High CV means very little or scanty rainfall. In parts of Saurashtra and Kutch, the CV of rainfall is 40-50% whereas in western Rajasthan it is 80-90%.
- Rainfall measuring device – ordinary and automatic/self-recording rain gauge.

Drought:

- Below 75% of the normal rainfall and severe drought when it is below 50%.

- In Indian history the year 1987 was recorded as the worst drought affected year followed by 2000.
- Palmer's drought Index is calculated with data on rainfall, ET and soil moisture.

Evapo-transpiration and Water balance:

- Evapo-transpiration = Evaporation from the soil surface + transpiration from plants.
- The extent to which the water needs of a crop are met in a locality depends on the rainfall input the losses due to run off and the evapo-transpiration.
- In India areas of high annual PET are extreme west of Rajasthan (Jaisalmer) and extreme south of Tamil Nadu (Tuticorin).
- Evaporation is determined using USWB Class A Open pan Evaporimeter.
- ET is measured using Lysimeters.

Temperature:

- Temperature is the degree of hotness of a substance.
- Lines joining places of equal temperature are called Isotherms.
- Sunshine is not a limiting factor in crop production any where in India.
- High humidity and warm temperatures are conducive to most plant pest and diseases.

Weather modification:

- Cloud seeding technique- Silver Iodide is used for cold clouds and sodium chloride is used for warm clouds.

General Points:

- Crop yield formulation is done using Regression Techniques.

- India has been divided into 15 Agro-climatic Zones.

Institutions Involved:

- Indian Institute of Tropical Meteorology
- India Meteorological Department (IMD), Pune, Maharashtra.
- Central Arid Zone Research Institute (CAZRI), Jodhpur, Rajasthan.
- International Crop Research Institute for semi-arid tropics (ICRISAT), Hyderabad, AP.
- National Centre for Medium Range weather Forecasting (NCMRWF), New Delhi.

Icar Institutions, Deemed Universities, National Research Centres,

The Indian Council of Agricultural Research (ICAR) is an autonomous organisation under the Department of Agricultural Research and Education (DARE), Ministry of Agriculture and Farmers Welfare , Government of India. Formerly known as Imperial Council of Agricultural Research, it was established on 16 July 1929 as a registered society under the Societies Registration Act, 1860 in pursuance of the report of the Royal Commission on Agriculture. The ICAR has its headquarters at New Delhi. The Council is the apex body for co-ordinating, guiding and managing research and education in agriculture including horticulture, fisheries and animal sciences in the entire country. With 111 ICAR institutes and 71 agricultural universities spread across the country this is one of the largest national agricultural systems in the world. The ICAR has played a pioneering role in ushering Green Revolution and subsequent developments in agriculture in India through its research and technology development that has enabled the country to increase the production of foodgrains by 5.6 times, horticultural crops by 10.5 times, fish by 16.8 times, milk by 10.4 times and eggs by 52.9 times since 1950-51 to 2017-18, thus making a visible impact on the national food and nutritional security. It has played a major role in promoting excellence in higher education in agriculture. It is engaged in cutting edge areas of science and technology development and its scientists are internationally acknowledged in their fields.

Deemed Universities - 4

1. ICAR-Indian Agricultural Research Institute, New Delhi
2. ICAR-National Dairy Research Institute, Karnal
3. ICAR-Indian Veterinary Research Institute, Izatnagar
4. ICAR-Central Institute on Fisheries Education, Mumbai

Institutions - 65

1. ICAR-Central Island Agricultural Research Institute , Port Blair
2. ICAR-Central Arid Zone Research Institute, Jodhpur

3. ICAR-Central Avian Research Institute, Izatnagar

4. ICAR-Central Inland Fisheries Research Institute, Barrackpore

5. ICAR-Central Institute Brackishwater Aquaculture, Chennai

6. ICAR-Central Institute for Research on Buffaloes, Hissar

7. ICAR-Central Institute for Research on Goats, Makhdoom

8. ICAR-Central Institute of Agricultural Engineering, Bhopal

9. ICAR-Central Institute for Arid Horticulture, Bikaner

10. ICAR-Central Institute of Cotton Research, Nagpur

11. ICAR-Central Institute of Fisheries Technology, Cochin

12. ICAR-Central Institute of Freshwater Aquaculture, Bhubneshwar

13. ICAR-Central Institute of Research on Cotton Technology, Mumbai

14. ICAR-Central Institute of Sub Tropical Horticulture, Lucknow

15. ICAR-Central Institute of Temperate Horticulture, Srinagar

16. ICAR-Central Institute on Post harvest Engineering and Technology, Ludhiana

17. ICAR-Central Marine Fisheries Research Institute, Kochi

18. ICAR-Central Plantation Crops Research Institute, Kasargod

19. ICAR-Central Potato Research Institute, Shimla

20. ICAR-Central Research Institute for Jute and Allied Fibres, Barrackpore

21. ICAR-Central Research Institute of Dryland Agriculture, Hyderabad

22. ICAR-National Rice Research Institute, Cuttack

23. ICAR-Central Sheep and Wool Research Institute, Avikanagar, Rajasthan

24. ICAR- Indian Institute of Soil and Water Conservation, Dehradun

25. ICAR-Central Soil Salinity Research Institute, Karnal

26. ICAR-Central Tobacco Research Institute, Rajahmundry

27. ICAR-Central Tuber Crops Research Institute, Trivandrum

28. ICAR-ICAR Research Complex for Eastern Region, Patna

29. ICAR-ICAR Research Complex for NEH Region, Barapani

30. ICAR-Central Coastal Agricultural Research Institute, Ela, Old

Goa, Goa

31. ICAR-Indian Agricultural Statistics Research Institute, New Delhi

32. ICAR-Indian Grassland and Fodder Research Institute, Jhansi

33. ICAR-Indian Institute of Agricultural Biotechnology, Ranchi

34. ICAR-Indian Institute of Horticultural Research, Bengaluru

35. ICAR-Indian Institute of Natural Resins and Gums, Ranchi

36. ICAR-Indian Institute of Pulses Research, Kanpur

37. ICAR-Indian Institute of Soil Sciences, Bhopal

38. ICAR-Indian Institute of Spices Research, Calicut

39. ICAR-Indian Institute of Sugarcane Research, Lucknow

40. ICAR-Indian Institute of Vegetable Research, Varanasi

41. ICAR-National Academy of Agricultural Research & Management, Hyderabad

42. ICAR-National Institute of Biotic Stresses Management, Raipur

43. ICAR-National Institue of Abiotic Stress Management, Malegaon, Maharashtra

44. ICAR-National Institute of Animal Nutrition and Physiology, Bengaluru

45. ICAR-National Institute of Natural Fibre Engineering and Technology, Kolkata, Kolkata

46. ICAR-National Institute of Veterinary Epidemiology and Disease Informatics, Hebbal, Bengaluru

47. ICAR-Sugarcane Breeding Institute, Coimbatore

48. ICAR-Vivekananda Parvatiya Krishi Anusandhan Sansthan, Almora

49. ICAR-Central Institute for Research on Cattle, Meerut, Uttar Pradesh

50. ICAR-National Institute of High Security Animal Diseases, Bhopal

51. ICAR-Indian Institute of Maize Research,Ludhiana

52. ICAR- Central Agroforestry Research Institute , Jhansi

53. ICAR-National Institute of Agricultural Economics and Policy Research, New Delhi

54. ICAR- Indian Institute of Wheat and Barley Research, Karnal

55. ICAR- Indian Institute of Farming Systems Research, Modipuram
56. ICAR- Indian Institute of Millets Research, Hyderabad
57. ICAR- Indian Institute of Oilseeds Research, Hyderabad
58. ICAR- Indian Institute of Oil Palm Research, Pedavegi, West Godawari
59. ICAR- Indian Institute of Water Management, Bhubaneshwar
60. ICAR-Indian Institute of Rice Research, Hyderabad
61. ICAR- Central Institute for Women in Agriculture, Bhubaneshwar
62. ICAR-Central Citrus Research Institute, Nagpur
63. ICAR-Indian Institute of Seed Science, Mau
64. ICAR-Indian Agricultural Research Institute, Post Box No. 48, Hazaribag 825 301, Jharkhand
65. ICAR-National Institute for Plant Biotechnology, New Delhi

National Research Centres - 14
1. ICAR-National Research Centre for Banana, Trichi
2. ICAR-National Research Centre for Grapes, Pune
3. ICAR-National Research Centre for Litchi, Muzaffarpur
4. ICAR-National Research Centre for Pomegranate, Solapur
5. ICAR-National Research Centre on Camel, Bikaner
6. ICAR-National Research Centre on Equines, Hisar
7. ICAR-National Research Centre on Meat, Hyderabad
8.. ICAR-National Research Centre on Mithun, Medziphema, Nagaland
9. ICAR-National Research Centre on Orchids, Pakyong, Sikkim
10. ICAR-National Research Centre on Pig, Guwahati
11. ICAR-National Research Centre on Seed Spices, Ajmer
12. ICAR-National Research Centre on Yak, West Kemang
13. ICAR-National Centre for Integrated Pest Management, New Delhi
14. Mahatma Gandhi Integrated Farming Research Institute ,Motihari

National Research Centres - 14
1. ICAR-National Research Centre for Banana, Trichi

2. ICAR-National Research Centre for Grapes, Pune

3. ICAR-National Research Centre for Litchi, Muzaffarpur

4. ICAR-National Research Centre for Pomegranate, Solapur

5. ICAR-National Research Centre on Camel, Bikaner

6. ICAR-National Research Centre on Equines, Hisar

7. ICAR-National Research Centre on Meat, Hyderabad

8.. ICAR-National Research Centre on Mithun, Medziphema, Nagaland

9. ICAR-National Research Centre on Orchids, Pakyong, Sikkim

10. ICAR-National Research Centre on Pig, Guwahati

11. ICAR-National Research Centre on Seed Spices, Ajmer

12. ICAR-National Research Centre on Yak, West Kemang

13. ICAR-National Centre for Integrated Pest Management, New Delhi

14. Mahatma Gandhi Integrated Farming Research Institute ,Motihari

National Bureaux - 6

1. ICAR-National Bureau of Plant Genetics Resources, New Delhi

2. ICAR-National Bureau of Agriculturally Important Micro-organisms, Mau, Uttar Pradesh

3. ICAR-National Bureau of Agricultural Insect Resources, Bengaluru

4. ICAR-National Bureau of Soil Survey and Land Use Planning, Nagpur

5. ICAR-National Bureau of Animal Genetic Resources, Karnal

6. ICAR-National Bureau of Fish Genetic Resources, Lucknow

Directorates/Project Directorates - 13

1. ICAR-Directorate of Groundnut Research, Junagarh

2. ICAR-Directorate of Soybean Research, Indore

3. ICAR-Directorate of Rapeseed & Mustard Research, Bharatpur

4. ICAR-Directorate of Mushroom Research, Solan

5. ICAR-Directorate on Onion and Garlic Research, Pune

6. ICAR-Directorate of Cashew Research, Puttur

7.. ICAR-Directorate of Medicinal and Aromatic Plants Research, Anand

8. ICAR-Directorate of Floricultural Research, Pune, Maharashtra

9. ICAR-Directorate of Weed Research, Jabalpur

10. ICAR-Project Directorate on Foot & Mouth Disease, Mukteshwar

11. ICAR-Directorate of Poultry Research, Hyderabad

12. ICAR-Directorate of Knowledge Management in Agriculture (DKMA), New Delhi

13. ICAR-Directorate of Cold Water Fisheries Research, Bhimtal, Nainital

The Commodity Committees

Year	Committee	Research station/ Institute
1921	Cotton committee	Technological laboratory now CTRL Matunga)
1931	Lac cess committee	Indian lac Research institute, Namkum (1936), Bihar
1936	Jute Committee	Jute Agricultural; Research institute, Barrakpore Jute Technological Research Laboratory, Calcutta, West bengal (Continues at Page 41)

COMMODITY COMMITTEES

State Agricultural Universities

Andhra Pradesh

1 Acharya NG Ranga Agricultural University, Guntur

2 Dr. YSRHU (APHU), Venkataramannagudem

3 Sri Venkateswara Veterinary University, Tirupati

Assam

4 Assam Agricultural University, Jorhat

Bihar

5 Bihar Agricultural University, Sabour, Bhagalpur

6 Bihar Animal Sciences University, Patna

Chhattisgarh

7 Indira Gandhi Krishi Viswa Vidhyalaya, Raipur

8 Chhattisgarh Kamdhenu Visvavidyalaya, Durg

Gujarat

9 Sardar Krushinagar Dantiwada Agricultural University, Dantiwada

10 Anand Agricultural University, Anand

11 Navsari Agricultural University, Navsari

12 Junagarh Agricultural University, Junagarh

13 Kamdhenu University, Gandhinagar

Haryana

14 Chaudhary Charan Singh Haryana Agricultural University, Hisar

15 Lala Lajpat Rai University of Veterinary & Animal Sciences, Hisar

16 Haryana State University of Horticultural Sciences, Karnal

Himachal Pradesh

17 Ch. Sarwan Kumar Himachal Pradesh Krishi Viswavidyalaya, Palampur

18 Dr. Yaswant Singh Parmar University of Horticulture & Forestry, Solan

Jharkhand

19 Birsa Agricultural University, Ranchi

Jammu & Kashmir

20 Sher-e-Kashmir University of Agricultural Science & Technology, Srinagar

21 Sher-e-Kashmir University of Agricultural Science & Technology, Jammu

Karnataka

22 University of Agricultural Sciences, Bangalore

23 Karnataka Veterinary, Animal and Fisheries Sciences University, Bidar

24 University of Agricultural Sciences, Raichur

25 University of Agricultural Sciences, Dharwad

26 University of Horticulture Science, Bagalkot

27 University of Agriculture & Horticulture Sciences, Shimoga

Kerala

28 Kerala Agricultural University, Thrissur

29 Kerala University of Fisheries and Ocean Studies, Panangad, Kochi

30 Kerala Veterinary and Animal Sciences University, Pookode, Wayanand, Kerala

Madhya Pradesh

31 Rajmata Vijayaraje Scindia Krishi VishwaVidyalaya, Gwalior

32 Nanaji Deshmukh Pashu ChikitsaVisvaVidyalaya, Jabalpur

33 Jawaharlal Nehru Krishi Viswa Vidyalaya, Jabalpur

Maharashtra

34 Dr. Balaesahib Sawant Kokan KrishiVidyapeeth, Dapoli

35 Maharastra Animal & Fisheries. Sciences University, Nagpur

36 Vasantrao Naik Marathwada Krishi Vidyapeeth, Parbhani

37 Mahatma Phule Krishi Vidyapeeth, Rahuri

38 Dr. Punjabrao Deshmukh KrishiViswaVidyalaya, Akola

Orissa

39 Orissa University of Agricultural & Technology, Bhubaneswar

Punjab

40 Guru Angad Dev Veterinary and Animal Sciences University, Ludhiana

41 Punjab Agricultural University, Ludhiana

Rajasthan

42 Maharana Pratap University of Agriculture & Technology, Udaipur

43 Swami Keshwanand Rajasthan Agricultural University, Bikaner

44 Rajasthan University of Veterinary & Animal Sciences, Bikaner

45 SKN Agriculture University, Jobner

46 Agriculture University, Kota

47 Agriculture University, Jodhpur

Tamil Nadu

48 Tamil Nadu Agricultural University, Coimbatore

49 Tamil Nadu Veterinary & Animal Sciences University, Chennai

50 Tamil Nadu Fisheries University, Nagapattinam

Telangana

51 Sri Konda Laxman Telangana State Horticultural University, Hyderabad

52 Sri PV Narsimha Rao Telangana Veterinary University, Hyderabad

53 Professor Jayashankar Telangana State Agricultural University, Hyderabad

UttraKhand

54 G.B. Pant University of Agriculture & Technology, Pantnagar

55 VCSG Uttarakhand University of Horticulture & Forestry, Bharsar

Uttar Pradesh

56 Chandra Shekhar Azad University of Agricultural & Technology, Kanpur

57 Narendra Deva University of Agriculture & Technology, Faizabad

58 Sardar Vallabhbhai Patel University of Agriculture & Technology, Meerut

59 U.P. Pt. Deen Dayal Upadhyaya Pashu Chikitsa VigyanVishwaVidhyalaya Evem Go Anusandhan Sansthan, Mathura

60 Banda University of Agricultural and Technology, Banda

West Bengal

61 Bidhan Chandra Krishi Viswa Vidhyalaya, Mohanpur

62 West Bengal University of Animal & Fishery Sciences, Kolkata

63 Uttar Banga Krishi Viswavidhyalaya, Cooch Behar

Varieties Of Important Crops

- **Rice TN-1 :** (First introduced drawf variety into India), IR-8, Jaya (Blast Resistant), Padma, Mashuri, Kakatiya, Pusa Basumati, Pusa Jaldidan, Lunisree, Ratna, TKM-6 (Stem borer resistant), Katdaribogh (Tungro resistant), ADT-27 (indica x japonica), Santchousong (High protein content), Dee-Gee-Woo-Gen, Bala (Drought resistant), IR-20 (Resistant to Blast, BLB, stemborer, leafhopper).
- **Wheat :** Introduction from Mexico: Lerma Rojo and sonara-64. Single gene dwarf varieties: Safed lerma, Sharbati sonara, pusa Lerma, Chotu lerma. Double gene dwarf varieties: Shera, Arjun, Janak. Triple gene dwarf varieties: Heera, Moti. HD series, Kundan, C-306 (drought resistant).

- **Chickpea:** Pusa 256 PBG-1 203, Pusa 209: Gaurav ICCC-32, Ajay.
- **Pigeonpea:** UPAS-120 9short duration), ICPH-8 (First Hybrid), (Arhar) Pusa 33. Pusa Agati, ICPL 37. Hira, Mukta, Bahar, Prabat. SBH-8.
- **Sugarcane: Noble Canes:** CO-419, Co-997
- **Soybean:** Bragg, Lee Clark-63, Shilajeet, Pusa 16, 20, 24, PK-327
- **Tomato:** Pusa Sheetal, Pusa-120, Pusa Early Dwarf, Pusa Ruby, Margologe, Sioux, Pusa Gauray, Best of All.
- **Mango:** Malika (neelam x dasheri) ~ Amrapali (dasheri x neelam) ~ Ratna (neelam x alphonso)

- **Bannana:** Poovan (larplur, Chakrakeli), Basrai, Champa ~ Hill Bananas: Sirumali, virupakshi ~ Culinary varieties: Monthan, Gross Mitchell, Mindoli Robusta Rasthali

- **Rose:** Chitra, Dr. B. P. Pal, Priyadarshini, Nehru Ceremony,

Jawhar, Abisarika, Banjara, Randhawa.

- **Califlower:** Pusa Deepali, Pusa synthetic, Pusa Katki, Early Snowball, Kanwari , Early, Patna, Patna Main crop, Snowball-16, Sutton's Snowball Japanese improved, Dania, Aghani, Poosi.

Fathers Of Different Disciplines

- Agronomy : Pietro Decrescenzi
- Agricultural chemistry : Justus von Liebig
- Antibiotics : Alexander Flemming
- ATP cycle : Lipmann
- Biology : Aristotle
- Botany : Theophrastus
- Bacteriology : Leuwenhoek
- Biochemistry : Justus von Liebig
- Cytology : Robert Hooke
- Cytoplasmic Inheritance : Carl Correns
- Cooperative movement in India : F. Nicholson
- DNA finger printing technique : Alec Jeffrey
- Economic Ecology : Dr. M.S Swaminathan
- Ecology : Reiter
- Extension Education : A. Seaman/ Leagnes
- Experimental Genetics : Thomas Hunt Morgan
- Forest pathology : Robert Haring
- Fermentation : Louis Pasteur
- Field plot experimentation : Jean Baptiste Boussingault

- Fruits and vegetables preservation : M. Nicolas Apart
- Genetics : Gregor Johann Mendel
- Genetic engineering : Paul Berg
- Green Revolution : Dr. N.E Borlaug
- Golden revolution in India : Dr. K.L Chadha
- Golden rice : Dr. Ingo Potrykus
- Hybrid Rice : Yuan Long Ping
- Hybrid cotton : C.T Patel
- Indian phytopathology : E.J Butler
- Indian Rust : Dr. K.C Mehta
- Indian Mycology : E.J Butler

- Indian Ecology : R. Mishra
- Indian plant breeding : Dr. B.P Pal
- Immunology : Edward Jenner
- Indian Green Revolution : Dr. M.S Swaminathan
- Microbiology : A.V Leuwenhoek
- Mycology : Pler A. Micheli
- Medicinal Bacteriology : Robert Koch
- Modern Genetics : T.H Morgan
- Mutation Theory : Hugo de vries
- Modern Botany : Linnaeus/ Bauchin
- Modern Cytology : Swanson
- Nematology : N. A Cobb
- Nitrogen Fixation : Winogradsky
- Ornamental Gardening : M.S Randhawa
- Plant Pathology : Anton De Bary
- Plant Physiology : Stephen Hales
- Pedology : VV Dokuchaev
- Parasitology : F. Platter
- Plant Tissue culture : G. Haberlandt
- Plant Anatomy : Grew
- Polygenic Inheritance : Kolreuter
- Pure culture technique : Oscar Brefeld
- Sociology : Auguste compte
- Statistics : R.A Fisher
- Soil Microbiology : S. N Winogradsky
- Soil testing Technique : M.L Troug
- Super Rice : Dr. G.S Khush
- Taxonomy : Carolus Linnaeus
- Tillage : Jethro Tull
- Virology : W.M Stanley
- Weeds : Jethro Tull
- White Revolution : Dr. Varghese Kurien
- Zoology : Aristotle
- Hybrid rice in India : E. A Siddiqe

Famous Name Of Crops

King of cereals : Wheat

Queen of cereals : Maize

King of fruits : Mango

Queen of fruits : Pineapple

King of temperate fruits : Apple

King of spices : Black Pepper

Queen of spices : Cardamom

Queen of vegetables : Potato

Poor man's meat : Soybean

Wonder crop : Soybean

Famine reserves : Millets

Camel of crops : Sorghum

Queen of oilseeds : Sesame

King of oilseeds : Mustard

Queen of fodder crops : Lucerne

King of fodder crops : Berseem

Poor man's fruit : Jackfruit, Ber

Vegetable meat : Cowpea

Poor man's substitute for ghee : Sesamum

Poor man's friend : Potato

Poor man's food : Pearl millet

King of arid and semi fruits : Ber

King of weeds : Congress grass (*Parthenium hysterophorus*)

National fruit of India : Mango

Glory of East : Chrysanthemum

Autumn queen : Chrysanthemum

Wonder tree : Neem

Queen of night : *Cestrum nocturnum*

Egg plant : Brinjal

Bio energy plant : Jatropha

Queen of flowers : Rose

Brown gold : Dead pupae of silkworm

Apple of paradise : Banana
Poor man's orange(India) and love of apple (England): Tomato
Drosophila of crop plants : Maize
Adams fig : Banana
Butter fruit : Avocardo
Queen of beverage crop : Tea
China's miracle fruit : Kiwi fruit
Food of god : Cocoa
Small holder's irrigated crop : Oil palm
Oldest cultivated tropical fruits : Banana
Tree of heaven : Coconut
King of coarse cereals : Sorghum

Terms And Associated Crops

Curing : Tobacco, Tea
    Stripping : Jute
    Nipping : Cotton
    Wrapping : Sugarcane
    Propping : Banana, sugarcane
    Trashing : Sugarcane
    Dapog seedling : Rice seedling
    De-suckering : Tobacco, Banana
    De-tasseling : Maize
    Pegging : Groundnut
    Retting : Jute
    Ginning : Cotton
    Tapping : Gram
    Staking : Tomato
    Arrowing : Sugarcane
    Rationing : Sugarcane
    Tipping : Tea